RELEASE ALL IN LOVE AND TRUST

MENTAL STRATEGIES WITH PHYSICAL SOLUTIONS

BY

HAVEN S. TURNER

ISBN: 978-1-7353219-0-5 (Paperback)

ISBN: 978-1-7353219-2-9 (eBook)

ISBN: 978-1-7353219-1-2 (Audio)

First edition published 2020

Contents

Kimora Is My Idol

To
Kimberly Antwinette Porter
Time Has Been Traded For Eternity
Now You Are Forever
Love Always,
Haven

INTRODUCTION

12/15/1970

Close to the eve of my four-year educational resignation, I was spending an evening relaxing in my home, when a massive venom, forced it's way to my universal surface. On this evening in particular, my mind was drawn away from my usual, eccentric, lingering's to the familiar ring of my cell. The name and number that appeared on the screen of my phone, revealed that it was my heart in the form of my Sister Friend. Delighted for the call, I answered with glee. Never did I imagine, she would utter words that would cause my soul to crack open and shatter to pieces.

"We have to start living our life, sis, Kim Porter has passed away at forty-seven years old!" Wordless silence escaped my dropped jaw. Once I gained some level of grounding, I allowed my soul to scream; there were no words, just moans and hollers. Initially resisting the cold and permanent reality of this truth, I defiantly told my Sister Friend, that I did not believe her and that I would not go online to find out. There was no need for me to do neither, the time arrived.

The Time Arrived

11/15/2018

Once I Released my own vain imaginings, I thought of Kim's four priceless children, and the host of friends and family that had the honor of sharing her space. The time arrived. My Release and the penning of this book was a few years in the making. I spoke of completion, carrying these remarkable words of wisdom, within my soul. Yet I allowed procrastination to take the task. The time arrived. As one of Kim Porter's followers on Instagram, I recalled a post she placed on her feed the year prior. With 2017 coming to a close, Kim's heart's desire rang true, when she posted a meme to the effect of, "I hope you receive your plot twist!" Almost a year later, the time arrived for me to take the gift of her life and share with the world how I was able to Release All In Love And Trust.

Through my news arrival, I vowed completion and dedication of my book to *Ms. Kimberly Antwinette Porter.* The dope, big sister, who's smile, through a portrait, penetrated my soul. Although I never had the pleasure of your warm embrace in this lifetime, I "will see you again, I'm sure of it!"

Weight Release is an endeavor and lifestyle where you will quickly grasp that your physical frame is matching your mental frame of mind. This vital discovery causes you to realize that in order to alleviate the barriers within your life, you have to *Release All In Love And Trust.*

As an example, for years, I held on to the belief that my obesity was caused by consuming unhealthy portions of nice and not-so-nice food. Pair that behavior with eating late and then going to sleep, shazaam!, you have my former figure. While those behaviors may surely lead to weight gain, the actions I took, were first due to my beliefs, the mental, what I was thinking upstairs, for my thoughts triggered my actions. When I began to recognize the low-vibrating transactions that devoured my mental, purging any contaminated thoughts and actions that no longer served me, became a priority.

Wouldn't you know, after paying attention and taking care of my mind, those once-stubborn, physical pounds melted off. To be transparent, my weight release path took place so rapidly, I reached bobble head status during the course of my journey and thought it best to put a couple of pounds back on -go figure. When you Release All In Love And Trust, you can also count on learning how to walk again. Yes, like a toddler's first wobbly steps, you will experience uncertainty in your early walking Release days. Think like a shaky leaf on a branch.

Weight Release requires a transformational shift, ripe, with oracles on your path. In order for a transformational shift to occur in my life, I embraced the words of several Truth Teachers throughout my Release. The first Truth Teacher is Florence Scovel Shinn, through the reading of her bio, I learned her nickname was Flossie, often I will follow suit and refer to her as the same. Dr. Joseph Murphy is another Light that reflected his love through words, his text *The Amazing Laws of Cosmic Mind Power* became my affirmation bible. Finally, but most certainly not least, is self-help and New Thought author Louise L. Hay. *You Can Heal Your Life*, is a reference book for me, one of my basic instructions before leaving earth. I encourage you to read this powerful text and do the same!

Let's Get Clique'

Here's what I want you to know, above all things **YOU CAN RELEASE YOUR MENTAL AND PHYSICAL WEIGHT!** The pictures and words you see on the following pages are real as well as living proof that you are able to Release any amount of weight you desire. Do not worry about the evil thoughts and bad days that may possibly come your way. This is just a sign from The Universe or your Higher Power that you are headed in the proper direction. The situation and circumstances you are facing are temporary, there is a lesson that must be learned. No matter how nasty the thoughts that surge in your mind, or gritty the beliefs you've held on to for your dear life, you are a Dope King or Queen. Most importantly, you are a Dope King or Queen that is able to **Release All In Love And Trust. I LOVE YOU!**

Chapter 1
Release All In Love & Trust

Release All In Love & Trust
Enough Was Enough

More than likely, if you are holding this book in your hands or through a technological platform, this experience has occurred in your life. We've all been there, our wobbly nerves, and shaky dance to the dressing room. While this process should not be daunting, it is! You are holding on to garments that may or may not lay on your curves in the manner that you desire. Thoughts of hope emerge from the recesses of your nervous, yet beautiful mind. The moment of truth feels heavy, about as light as a boulder, yet it is a task that you endure over and over again. Yes! I do mean endure! Garment after garment, dress after dress. Each piece of denied clothing feeling more like a rejection to our soul rather than body.

One of my most memorable, pre-weight Release moments I can recall was attempting to try on a unique dress in a major department store. My eyes and heart feigned for the dress, however, I felt on my body, it would be taking a chance. As I began to slip the garment over my head and down to my shoulders, well, that's about as far as the dress was received on my then frame. Let me get to where enough was enough, in the midst of my dressing room defeat, I had to remove the dress. What do you know? The beautiful garb would not go up nor down-STUCK! What feelings of frustration and rejection-AGAIN! After clamoring for help, aka, my mother to the rescue, the dress felt like it had to be extracted, like a wisdom tooth, from my body. This experience was one too much. The pangs of my mind, soul, and body cried out to be Released.

What You Lose You Will Find
Lost & Found

For many years, obesity was a place, I called home, it wasn't that I loved this home or that it was a safe haven to live and visit, however it was home. Emotional eating and a lack of self-love was a lifestyle, and since my eating habits reflected my lifestyle I had to let go of all the fallacious notions I harbored.

I cannot recall where I heard the term "what you lose, you will find", however those words of wisdom were like adhesive to my soul. Here's an analogy that allowed me to make a shifting connection. Do you remember the "lost and found", consider it's purpose? One of the intentions or purpose of a lost and found is to provide a space, to help one, recover items that may have been left, misplaced, or found by another individual. A lost and found is a supposed drop-off setting, should you stumble upon someone else's valuables. Not only is the lost and found for you to drop off lost items, it is also a place for those who lost something to seek.

Here is where we can get into trouble, and not trouble with eating unhealthy food that can lead to being overweight. You may consistently be accessing the lost and found within your life, yes, YOUR LIFE! Before you head over to the lost and found with your life, please take a moment to consider what you believed you lost, and most importantly if it needs to be found. Here's the thing, worry, doubt, shame, fear, unworthiness, non-supportive friends and family, need to remain lost. The critical step in this lost and found piece is YOU. You my dear friend have to mentally Release that which was "lost".

That's why there was a lost and found in our lives to begin with, we were losing things under the impression that we were supposed to find them again. Real life occurrences, like obesity and grief, do not go and find them. These low vibrations have to be Released not found. Did you lose your smile, go find that? Did you lose your sense of direction, go find that?

However, today, and for the rest of your life, you are a Releaser. When negative people and comments head your way, Release them, when past events keeps you stymied in your feelings, Release All In Love And Trust. Why, because when you decide to be a Releaser and not a loser, you discover, there is nothing to go and find only Release. By choosing to Release you are granting yourself access for your hearts desires to be fulfilled.

Now that you are a Releaser, this powerful lifestyle strategy applies to physical pounds as well. You do not lose weight, you Release it! Words do have power and are triggered from our thoughts. Let's not savor, tasteless thoughts. Knowing, believing, and trusting that all is being Released, not lost, will have you gliding into a bodycon dress or making someone's day, rocking a pair of Levi's. A quick Amazon.com search for weight loss books, revealed a whopping 30,000 results. Remember, "what you lose you will find", and we are not wasting our lives finding a weight loss journey again and again. No, no, no, we've switched it up and *Release All In Love And Trust.*

This is my favorite pic to show to drop peoples jaw with my weight
Release

Thank You For Flying Release Airlines
Please Place Your Trays in the Upright Position

Welcome aboard Release Airlines! As we prepare for takeoff please place your trays in the upright position, fasten your seatbelts, and stow all luggage in the overhead bin or beneath your seat. During this flight, you will experience turbulence, drops in cabin pressure, and the occasional bumps, knocks, and knicks, from your fellow passengers, their children, and our beautiful staff in the form of airline stewards. As always, enjoy your flight, and thank you for flying with Release Airlines.

Now that we have prepared for takeoff, travel with me for a moment. Envision an airplane as well as airplanes, taking off at an airport. For instance, "at Hartsfield-Jackson International Airport, one plane leaves about every 37 seconds, with destinations to over 50 countries and 75 international locations". Your subconscious is like an airplane, boarded to capacity with beliefs. Good, bad, or indifferent, these beliefs, like airplanes at Hartsfield-Jackson International Airport, lift off, every moment, reaching the final destination of their thought. Who is the pilot of your beliefs, does your co-pilot believe in the same values? What are the thoughts of your flight attendants and crew? Where are the passengers in the airplanes of your subconscious mind headed?

Subconscious S'more (Some More)

Naturally, one wonders, and wants to know, what in the hell is a *subconscious*. An example I found most comprehensible states, "*The subconscious stores all of your memories, beliefs, previous experiences, the people/places you have seen, and the skills you have acquired. Information in the subconscious cannot be recalled easily, they are buried deep within our minds (or repressed)."* By way of illustration, when you travel on an airline, your subconscious mind grants you the ability to complete the instructions requested by the airline steward or stewardess.

House of Mirrors

The fun does not stop there with your subconscious, how about this house of mirrors? BrianTracy.com states "by the time you reach the age of 21, you've already permanently stored more than one hundred times the contents of the entire *Encyclopedia Britannica.*" For those of us old enough to remember, draw from your memory bank, those old school sets of encyclopedias', they were colossal in nature. Built from firm binding, Encyclopedia Britannica had quality hardcovers, and hundreds of glossy pages filled with amazing research. This analogy is nothing to prance around, while 21 will still find you young and dumb, emphasis on both, you have a feast of experiences and beliefs your subconscious devours all times of the day, we'll call it a 24/7 gift. Which transition's perfectly to my next thought – a belief.

All the Believers in the House Make Some Noise

Shalashabe! Sha-la-sha-be –that was a belief known exclusively to myself and older brother, as a helicopter or airplane. While the origin of this term was never discovered, it was a tenacious belief we gripped and held fast to. Sidebar, I do not remember at what age we made the switch, obviously it was fast enough, I don't remember it coming up in counseling, (wink). Here's the coolest definition of belief I found at ChangingMinds.org, "belief is an assumed truth."

Yes and yikes! Please believe in progressive substances, however, you will learn, assumption causes us to experience ample airplane crashes in our lives personally and professionally. To draw from the Shalashabe example, let's say I continued to hold on to the belief that Shalashabe was the name of an airplane or helicopter. Just imagine the opposition and lack of peace that would have come my way clinging to an "assumed truth". Imagine if you were the customer service agent with whom I needed to book a ticket, "Hello Release Airlines, I would love to book a first class ticket on one of your finest Shalashabe's" or even better, explaining to your friends or family, "my Shalashabe lands at 9:45 this morning, please don't keep me waiting." PathwaytoHappiness.com declares "there's multiple parts to a belief, the way its constructed in our mind. We're not trained to notice it, so it takes a bit of work to separate them out with clarity." While humor may be the pull and tidbit I exhausted for this case, all can easily book a flight headed to our more complex beliefs. The beliefs that have me writing this book through experience and you reading it, the beliefs we have to Release in Love and Trust.

"That's A Problem, You're Not the Problem"

Complex, low-vibrating beliefs causes delays in our flights. Who here has boarded a plane, to taxi the runway for what seemed like an eternity? Let's not forget to include last minute gate switching and 2-hour layovers. Least I fail to mention, the ever-talking, weirdo passenger, that guide us along on what seems like majority of our flights. Oh my dear friends, belief is the ultimate flight and here's why all your systems need to be cleared for take-off, "you may be operating with a system of beliefs that are negative, false, fear-based and that's a problem, but you're not the problem."

"The 2 Most Crucial Phases of a Flight – Take-off and Landing."

"V1"

"V1"

While this is a term that airline passengers do not hear, it's a signal that all pilots and crew members alike love to hear. V1- is an aircraft's clearance for take-off, "beyond this velocity, the aircraft cannot be safely stopped on the ground and must become airborne". Consider the "V1" signal, as a thought based on our beliefs, and those beliefs take off once the plane -our thoughts, hit "100 knots or 115 mph". Yes, this is the velocity and speed with which airplanes and what you are thinking, are cleared for take-off. Let us all take time to consider the thoughts we are thinking. Are these thoughts, as fast and as mighty as they are, one that you would want the Universe to respond too? Not all my thoughts deserve deliverance, and hindsight allows you to see why you were not given clearance for takeoff with those thoughts and beliefs.

"You Need Clearance for Take-Off"

Like the mechanics and intricacy of an aircraft, we humans, are fearfully and wonderfully made, our thoughts can scream danger or calmly tell us to move along rapidly. Yet, just like aircrafts, our beliefs and thoughts NEED clearance for take-off. Pause. Be still. You can determine your V1 thoughts by doing so.

"Are these beliefs, preparing for take-off, highly vibrating to a speed of 115 mph or 100 knots?"

If no, these thoughts need to be released instantly to dry and arid places. You must know, this Release of non V1 thoughts needs to be completed in love and trust, we are Releasing issues and hurts to the generations. There is no one to blame for those low-vibrational thoughts, not even yourself, immediately dismiss those generational curses by using the following affirmation:

I now release by my spoken word, any low-vibrating thoughts or beliefs, "known and unknown, real and imagined, in all directions of time and space". Feel free to adjust the affirmation to fit your needs and personal culture. Remember there is no right or wrong with affirmations, you just want to clear the negative out in a loving and assured tone, with a firm belief in the affirmation.

Post Weight Release Halloween Costume – A Butterfly

Cool Tip to Remain Faithful

Spray Perfume to Lighten Your Mood

Let me be the first to tell you, that just because you have read this book and applied these strategies as lifestyle, you will still have those low-vibrating days and thoughts. Anybody who tells you different is a liar - run fast away from them, those are not your people. However, because those reasonings and days arise, we do not have to go it alone. Spray perfume to lighten your mood! In an article titled "The Hidden Force of Fragrance", the author states "scents can have positive effects on mood, stress reduction, sleep enhancement, self-confidence and physical and cognitive performance. By becoming more aware of the way specific odors affect you personally, you may be able to enhance your health."

Spraying perfume is endearing to me, I adore mixing scents. I become Tinker Bell and explore lands to my imaginings. Mixing scents also allows you to add variety, take a moment and explore the lands of your vision and fantasies, yesssss! Let me create my own sampler platter, using my frame as a muse!

Perfume Hacks

Since I mentioned perfume, here are some cool perfume hacks I discovered.

- "Rub Vaseline on your pulse points before spraying your perfume to make the scent last longer. The ointment, which is occlusive, will hold the fragrance to your skin longer than if you were to spray it onto dry skin." FYI-this is a common perfume hack that

I ran across on several websites.

- "Target pulse points and warm areas on your body when spraying perfume. To make your scent last longer, choose a couple target areas (not all of them at once) to spritz. The warm areas indicated will help diffuse the fragrances across your entire body and spraying your ankles and calves will allow the scent to rise throughout the day."

- "Pour the last bit of fragrance from an almost-empty perfume bottle into unscented lotion so nothing goes to waste." This hack is a gem for me, I'm one of those people who can't let those last 2-3 sprays in the bottle go, I spray, push, and maneuverer the bottle until all its content have disappeared. Another reason I enjoy this perfume tip because it pushes me in the direction of being clutter free.

- Familiarize yourself with common fragrance terms so you know exactly what the sales associates are referring to when helping you find a new perfume. Here are some sweet aroma terms:

  » Bergamot – "Essential oil from the rind of the Citrus Aurantium, an inedible fruit that looks like a small orange."

  » Amber – "There is no amber ingredient in the wild. Amber is the cornerstone accord of Oriental fragrances."

  » Accord – "An accord is a scent made up of several perfume notes, or ingredients, that blend together to form a distinct fragrance." Think of a brand who's perfume you love, what accords do they use to mix and create your favorite scent?

- "To make your fragrances last longer store them in cool, dark, places. Heat, light, and humidity breaks down the essence of your perfumes and over time diminish its quality. Instead of storing your perfumes on or around your bathroom sink, place perfumes in your room away from a window." I love this tip because it protects the overall investment you made into your toiletries. While the bulk of my perfume will be stored in this fashion, I keep a couple of bottles in my restroom, near the soap and lotion, for my female guest to enjoy post bathroom, Lord knows that situation can get sticky

- "Use the right type of perfume for longevity. Understanding perfume concentrations might help you with picking out the best longevity of a scent. Fragrances with the highest concentration of oil last longer with just a spritz. For instance, eau de parfums contain 15-20 percent of essential oils which lasts up to 4-5 hours making them costlier compared to eau de toilettes and colognes, which only has 5-15% of essential oils and can last up to 2-3 hours."

Take Time

While this may not be a common practice to yourself or anyone you know, please take the time to investigate what scents mix well with your body's chemical balances. You can invest in the finest colognes and perfumes, nevertheless if it does not blend with the essence of who you are, as an individual, within your soul, you will experience an epic fail in the scent department. Ultimately leaving your investment unused or doubling as air spray freshener. To better assist you in selecting the proper scents, "get a fragrance with long-lasting base notes. You might want to consider choosing a perfume with a woodsy base note as they tend to have better staying power. Scents with citrus base notes tend to disappear the fastest."

Smell A Sale

Keep in mind the times of year, when your beloved store has their annual and semi-annual sales, use this time and sale to stock up on your scents, bearing in mind the information you learned about perfumes. Don't forget to access the internet and mailbox for coupons to increase your savings!

Meditation Time & Not

Fact: "You can use your sense of smell to deliver instant relaxation. Pick a distinctive odor, then pair that aroma with a calming meditation session. After a few sessions, the odor itself will elicit a relaxed state, even when you don't have time to meditate."

Praise Him Anyhow
"Just Can't Leave It Alone"

Now that I mentioned the approach of spraying perfume, to not go it alone, it sparked this tried and true personal experience within me I can't leave alone. Dark days and complex thoughts can be turned on their head and viewed through the lenses of gratitude, a paradigm shifter. Here's why you experience those low vibe days and complex thoughts, you no longer accept negative thoughts as the norm, you no longer accept as true you are not worthy of the goodness of the Universe. In fact, you know you are worthy to receive and He called you out of darkness into His own marvelous light. Your subconscious is saying hell no, you don't live here anymore, my residence temple is occupied and overflowing with high-vibrating thoughts, you got to go! Praise yourself and your Higher Power for acknowledging that these thoughts are not you and they produce a life that you do not want. Praise Him because your conscious and subconscious are vigilantly declaring a positive battle and you are winning, because the battle has been won, you are saying to yourself and soul, "no more, you are a thought that is not real and I dismiss the very belief of you"!

Please Remember

Just as sure as you must have some form of physical activity to experience long term weight release and prepare for war by boot camp and training, the mental battle with your heart, mind, and soul, is of equivalent combat to be truly Released.

"The Hardest Part is Letting Go"
-Selena (1997)

Totally bonding with the motion picture Selena, my next career stop was singing and dancing-despite not being able to hold a note with a handle and two left feet attached to those tone-deaf notes. At a certain junction in the film, Selena herself, was dared to take the plunge and bungee jump. After accepting the dare and atop the bungee jumping station, Selena takes a panoramic view of the scene below and links it to her life. It was then that the machine operator unwittingly told Selena "the hardest part is letting go". Using the words of the operator as a metaphor to her life, Selena releases the handles and successfully bungee jumps.

Overthinking, worry, and unbelief will create commotion, disorder, and unrest during your flight. Yes, resistance to not letting go, will cause that annoying passenger, who takes up your seat and theirs up, to rise, not to mention, the 3-month-old with colic to be sitting right behind you. Oh yes, while the hardest part may be letting go, by NOT doing so, you create adverse weather conditions which ensures a turbulent flight better known as your life.

The Airplane of Belief Has Taken Off
Here's What You Need to Do
•NOTHING•

Now that we have reached the proper altitude, here's what you're to do – NOTHING! We've learned through experience, what happens when we don't let go. An illustration you, nor I, wouldn't dream of, is asking the pilot or co-pilot you are flying with, to step aside while you man the flight. No, you remain comfortable and quiet in your seat and leave the pilot and crew to their job. A Chinese proverb states "the philosopher leaves the cut of his coat to the tailor". The same applies with our beliefs and thoughts, they have taken off, you must trust the process, trust that your flight and crew are doing their job and working on your behalf.

Here's but one of the countless reasons why you need not do a thing. Known to many as a "breather hole", visualize that tiny hole that is in every window seat on an airplane. A breather hole "allows pressure to balance between the passenger cabin and the air gap, and releases moisture from the air gap, preventing the window from fogging up or frosting over." Your Higher Power has you covered, He/She, is on their job and definitely aware of your needs and wants. When I am experiencing some mental stickiness or thoughts that are not of V1 clearance, I lean on the King James version of Isaiah 65:24 *"And it shall come to pass, that before they call, I will answer; and while they are yet speaking, I will hear."* Yes, Haven and fellow Releasers, your Higher Power or Pilot of your Flight has you covered, so much so, that He/She "answered before you even called". Think of this truth when you are wrestling with thoughts of anxiety and anger. Embrace this truth and reality by forming this verse into your own affirmation, doing so offers a powerful connection of truth and meaning to your life.

Your Oxygen Mask May Deploy

Taking a trip to a new destination will naturally ignite feelings of excitement, do not let these feelings overcome you and trick you into believing that you can handle the flight and its intricacies from here, remember, leave the cut of your coat to the tailor. Remember assumption causes turbulence and plane crashes. "No matter who you meet along the way or what, stay locked in".

Don't Open That Door

Have you ever heard of hypoxia? There's a strong chance you will experience "a lack of oxygen, which leads to sluggish thinking, dimmed visions, unconsciousness and then death" when you begin to interfere with the job of the flight crew. This is but one of the effects caused when you open the plane door during a flight, aka, once your V1 thoughts have taken off, you interfere with negative thoughts and overthinking, not Releasing. The fun does not stop there when you pry open the cabin door, "the cabin temperature would quickly plummet to frostbite-inducing levels, and the plane itself might even begin to break apart".

And Action!

Here's the thing about life, when we all begin to think and act like we can do our life better than our Higher Power, we turn into actors or circus performers, we jump through rings of fire, play a character from a dark film, and last but not least find ourselves as a polar bear riding a tricycle. Buddy, it gets ugly when you interfere, you're kicking, fighting, sweating, your palms and brows are covered with perspiration, but guess what, YOU CAN'T OPEN THE DOOR IF YOU WANTED TO!!! "Cabin pressure won't allow, at a typical cruising altitude, up to eight pounds of pressure are pushing against every square inch of interior fuselage. That's over 1,100 pounds against each square foot of door". Your Higher Power knows the plans He/She has for you, get out of the way, Release interference -it's a must and enjoy your flight!

Start Here

If you notice your thoughts are not where they need to be, start here. A baby step instance to extinguish negatives beliefs and thoughts, would be to pick your least busiest day of the week and your least resistant time of the day (i.e. not after work and you're headed to daycare to pick up the kids) and be ever vigilant in examing and controlling your thoughts. Another quick affirmation to destroy those false thoughts is by saying "not so". Learned from Rev. Dr.

Michael Bernard Beckwith, "not so" has been a great tool to access when I am in those situations where I am unable to cry out, such as, being at work completing a task that requires me to be a team player, "not so" would have to be my words for the day. Perhaps reflections of the past, place you, your mind, body, and soul into a low vibrating scenario. Reacting to all the shoulda, woulda, coulda, and next time he or she does that, I will do this and that. To all of it "Not So" and/or "God is With Me". Immediately reach for these free resources, you will soon find that your entire world shifts with these new beliefs.

Side Note

"If I could do it all over again" spews toxins into your current system. Repeat, a past situation, no man ever – alive or dead – can take back or do it over again. When you hit replay to those past low vibrating situations, you are wreaking havoc into your current system.

Be S.M.A.R.T.
Set A Goal

"If you aim at nothing, you will hit it every time."
-Zig Ziglar

Releasing, growing, and healing will have you hearing and reclaiming your heart's desire. Inside the barracks of your heart lives dreams and desires to be fulfilled. One method to achieve these desires is by setting a goal. Why a goal? Goals are "the oxygen to our dreams". Reminisce on times when you aimlessly uttered that you were going to complete a task, put some stamps in your passport, read a book, complete an online course, run 3 times a week, etc., how far did you get with that, probably about the same as me? Hence why goal setting is essential, it maintains the focus. You notice how I used the word "aimlessly"? That is often what we do mentally with a commission that's floating about in our soul - no direction or aim. "Goal setting provides you the foundation for your drive".

As an expert Life Coach, one method of execution that I recommend to others is setting a S.M.A.R.T. Goal. "A SMART goal clarifies exactly what is expected and the measures used to determine if the goal is achieved and successfully completed."

The acronym for **SMART** is:

- S – Specific & Strategic

- M – Measurable

- A – Attainable/Achievable

- R – Relevant & Realistic

- T – Time Bound

Land

Given the state of the topic – minding and monitoring your beliefs, lets create a SMART goal within this realm. I have created the following, please remember you can modify this goal, like affirmations, according to your schedule and personality.

SMART Goal:

On each Tuesday, for the month of December, I will closely examine and control my thoughts from the hours of 9 a.m. to 10 a.m., when a negative thought or belief surfaces, I will use the affirmation/strategy "Not So" or "God is With Me" to release the negative thought. Should I forget this time and space, I will not lose a limb or organ, however I will go on to select another time frame within that day to closely examine and control my thoughts. To safeguard that I complete this SMART goal, my co-worker will be my accountability partner for those days and time.

Release Reminder Wrap Up

- Examine your beliefs or "assumed truth"

- Your thoughts emerge based off belief, that's what's taking off

- How many different thoughts are you thinking? What thoughts need to be replaced with airplanes of truth, headed toward destinations of peace?
  Here's a calming affirmation to restore peace during those moments. "My thoughts of truth, are NOW, reaching my destinations of peace."

- Send out higher vibrations through thought, movement, and sincere action – What was your favorite song in the 5th grade? Find that song on YouTube or download it from iTunes and rock out to it alone

- Tell yourself a joke that no one else finds funny but you, "Why did the one-eyed teacher close down the school? Because he only had one pupil? HA HA HA! Hey, I remember it from the 3rd grade!

Yes! This photo is proof that you are able to Release your weight!

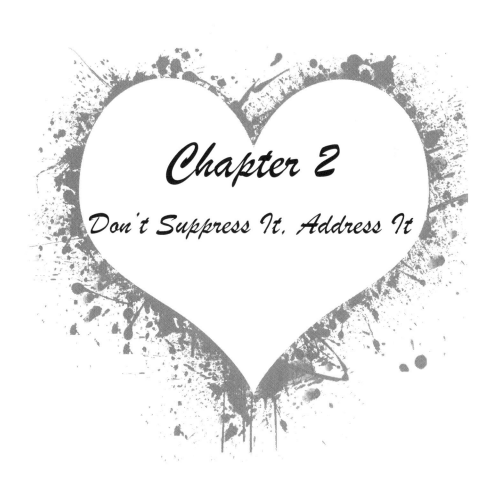

Chapter 2

Don't Suppress It, Address It

Don't Suppress It, Address It!

"Once upon a time", remember the constant lure you received in fairy tales alike? Drawing your senses into a mythical world contained with wizards, talking animals and life lessons to be learned. As far as I can remember, we're taught the same lure in regard to our emotions with our lives. Yes, we are taught well to hide and suppress our emotions. An example is when we were younger, with our spongy-minded selves and our well-being was the responsibility of an elder. During these formative years and experiences, we unconsciously duplicate how we were taught (or not) to address our emotions.

Instead of examining our feelings, we trudge along, suppressing colossal emotions. Suppressing our emotions, thoughts, or feelings, causes the silencing of our voice – our true selves. *One definition of suppress at Google.com defines suppress as "forcibly put an end to" with synonyms like "repress, crush, squash, and stamp out!"* Please raise your hand or holler out if you want any of these vocabulary words to be the adjectives that describe your life. I'm not raising my hand nor hollering out! Over at FitLife.tv, Doris Dahdouh explains, "When you deny yourself the right to be expressive, you can do serious damage not only to your mind and soul, but also to your physical body." Here's the catch, majority of those emotions are fraudulent, purely counterfeit, and create "toxic sludge in the plumbing of your subconscious mind."

Ditch the Suppress
Soul Suppress

Bestselling author and my spiritual development coach, Debrena Jackson-Gandy explained a soul suppress to me in the following example. Your "Girlfriend" framed in her most expensive bodycon dress and adorned in her finest Kendall Miles, black stilettos, accidently lands one of those spiked heels on your big toe. Yikes! "Girlfriend" immediately apologizes and tends to your wellbeing. Regardless of the apology and accident, your soul and big toe are in absolute pain. The misstep has sent a shrieking pain up your spine.

Here's where we would previously soul suppress, and say "it's ok, I'm fine, don't worry, I was probably walking to fast anyhow" (as women that list can go on and on). While the facts remain what they are – an accident - we suppressed our own pain that is literally crying out to be addressed. Be clear, not in the addressing form of belittling yourself or your friend. Just do not deny your soul. Heroically say to your humanity and body, "that hurt me, really, really, hurt me!" This step is critical because *you have to be at peace with addressing your pain.* Take the leap, be brave enough to stand up for yourself and say, "I am having a human experience that caused temporary pain, and that is perfectly fine to address!"

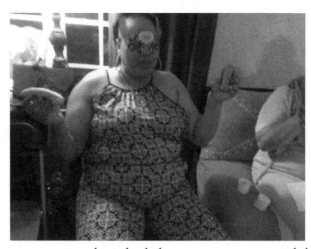

Here I am at my co-worker's bachelor party, pregnant with hurt, anger, and fear.

Mind Suppress

"Sticks and stones may break my bones, but words will never hurt me" – WRONG! Words are the sticks and stones that may break your bones. Reminiscence on an event in your life, where you experienced negative emotions. Often, a wintry, exchange, thought or belief initiated the unwanted emotion. To further explain, think of the physical reaction you have to unsolicited comments. For me, I clinch my hands in frustration, my head may begin to hurt, and flashes of experiences (sometimes with the same individual), that trigger these same emotions, emerge in my mind. Nooo! We no longer have to suppress our response to unwanted, less desirable circumstances. While you have absolutely no control over anyone else, you can have perfect (perfect meaning subjective) control of yourself. "If you allow an emotion to exist for 90 seconds, without judging, it will disappear." Say huh, say who, say what? Yes, ever thought 90 seconds would sound and feel so delicious, it's an excellent splurge to indulge in?!

Dr. Jill Bolte Taylor, author of My Stroke of Insight, is the soul that shared this life-changing approach. As you read her words below, trust, it works! Time after time, I have found myself immersed in towering emotions, by acknowledging my right and gift to 90 seconds, those emotions totally phase out. Guess what else I discovered? You don't need the entire 90 seconds!!! Yes, when I acknowledge, aka say to myself, its o.k., you have 90 seconds, its as if I have snapped my finger or flipped a light switch on, the emotion or emotions being experienced totally evaporates or becomes minuscule in nature, causing the seamless flow of my life to resume. Take a peek!

"Something happens in the external world and chemicals are flushed through your body which puts it on full alert. For those chemicals to totally flush out of the body it takes less than 90 seconds. This means that for 90 seconds you can watch the process happening, you can feel it happening, and then you can watch it go away."

Physical Body Suppress

We have addressed what suppression looks like on a soul level, even explored the results on a mind level; let us saunter over to your beautiful internal physique. "You have digestive problems. According to PowerofPositivity.com, from upset stomach and ulcers to acid reflux and constipation; there are many digestive problems caused by suppressed emotions." Let's turn our attention to the words "digestive problems". In effect, you become "backed-up". We all, at one time or another have taken residence in this place. As

27

an analogy, picture and recall, major city traffic, a post-office line, or the mandatory, license renewal, take a number line. These instances and numerous others can gradually become backed-up. When we continue to suppress our emotions, we are taking all those common denominators and plunging them down our insides or as I stated earlier, our beautiful internal physique. So, there's no surprise at all with our swelling thighs or bulging belly, there is an effect to every cause. Inspect your causes, what is their effect, do they lead to suppression? Toting abrasive thoughts around definitely will create a pool of repression. However, divorcing those hazardous thoughts and establishing a union where addressing is the right-of-way, we will then observe complete transformation within our lives.

I Now Present You the Gift of Taking a Moment

There is something of upmost importance that I must address. There has been a lot to chew as well as digest within this slice - which is why there is something I must address! Give yourself the gift of taking a moment. YOU WILL STILL FEEL LOW VIBRATIONS (anger, worry, resentment) or as if, you are in the pits of hell. Here's why you need that beautiful, luscious moment-IT'S O.K. TO FEEL THAT WAY, TAKE AND DEMAND YOUR 90 SECONDS! Do not linger in those emotions, its hell there for YOU, all of that shit and muck returns to the sender. I, Haven Turner, implore you to give yourself this gift. Trust me, I have spent entire days lugging barrels of expired emotional weight on my human shoulders, when a moment was simply available. Let that feeling, thought, or past event, just slide right through you, by taking the gift of a moment.

To establish a true, sound, meaning within our subconscious for "taking a moment" let us make a hand to pen connection, in your Release workbook, write the following affirmation down three times, with the last affirmation being written in cursive.

I now give myself the gift of taking a moment.

I now give myself the gift of taking a moment.

I now give myself the gift of taking a moment.

Por que with handwriting? The benefits are tranquil and appetizing, "writing by hand stimulates a part of the brain called the RAS, or the Reticular Activating System. RAS prioritizes what requires immediate focus and filters other out. Writing activates your RAS to process knowledge into your memory. Studies have shown children's brains were stimulated much more when asked to write down words in their notebooks rather than simply focusing on them." Another delicious slice to writing by hand is that, not only will your mind bolt to the rescue and focus on what matters- the addition of cursive, "can really help kickstart your brain again, by doing so, you are coordinating the brain's hemispheres."

From Me to You

We are ever evolving, and no matter where you may be in your development (seconds, minutes, hours, days, weeks, months, years), you will experience L-I-F-E! No matter how much I attempt to resist its ebb and flow, it's a fact attached to a beautiful truth. An affirmation to guide you through these stages would be, "There is an anointing of ease on my life! There is an anointing of ease on my life! There is an anointing of ease on my life!"

Delicious Address

We can dance, dance, dance
Clap your hands, hands, hands

-*Faith Evans*

Here's the splendid address! There's a delectable portion to Releasing All in Love And Trust. YOU READY? You do not have to suppress your taste buds for food! You read correctly, not only do you NOT suppress your taste buds for food, you address them in a delicious, exquisite, and palatable way!! Doesn't that make you want to "Do a little dance, make a little love, get down tonight"! Leaning on the experience of my mother's weight release journey, this savory technique, kept me from binge eating as well as aided in relinquishing patterns of old, wink twice if you have eaten when you were not hungry. I'll wink twice for you, cause it's for damn sure been me. There is nothing wrong with craving and indulging in some mouthwatering cheesecake with cherries on top, release that form of suppression. By the way, you will automatically release overeating, by making this a healthy, lifestyle habit. In other words, devour succulent dishes and enchanting entree's, nevertheless, address and exercise portion control. We'll get to her – "Portion Control" in just a few!

Beckoning Call

Clarity is a must at this junction in our Release Road, we have received vital data and information that pertain to our lives, so I MUST BE CLEAR. I am not stating eat HOWEVER you want, but whatever you want. Eating foods high in sodium and sugar, such as fast food daily, we can clearly see the physical results. Case in point, as a former classroom educator, your days can become endless, believe me, you can take a 12-hour workday on the chin like its nothing. Living that lifestyle, guess what delicatessen I raced to post quitting time-Chinese food? Otherwise known as the monster of fast food, the mega mouth of death. I could not devour enough fried chicken, smother my face and shirt in fried rice, and dare I not be stingy and chop down, in 1 or 2 bites, a fried egg roll! Mercy! Essentially, I was pulling up to a gas station, like my car, and filling my body up with octane's equivalent, sometimes to the point of overflow. With analogies as such being representative of our lives, we must live distinguishable by renouncing suppression. WOO HOO!

Let's get festive with receiving that superb news, do the Cha-Cha Slide, maneuver into the Cabbage Patch, and find yourself doing the Texas Hop, you MUST rejoice that you no longer suppress your taste buds for food, now it's a scrumptious, luscious address. Let's celebrate!!!!

Before I Let GoActivity:
Put On a Construction Worker Hat

Put on a construction worker hat, the plastic type, designed for kids, you know! Check the Dollar Tree before heading to Dillard's or a fine department store. ;). As we spoke of earlier, you will have your days and moments where low vibrations arise, here's the solution. When the space and environment allow, throw on your construction worker hat and address all those unwanted feelings. When asked why the construction worker hat, reply "under construction, I'm addressing, not suppressing!"

Please Remember

- 90 Seconds To Go - Please remember to use your 90 seconds! We are all works-in-progress, brighten the healing process by grasping "growth through joyous experience" in my Abraham Hicks voice. Your aim is to evolve and add benefits to the cypher of your life. Take a moment and allow the emotion(s) to pass through your body. Once this approach becomes who you are, you will be the much-needed "positive motivating force" within your life. Which is one of the goals to *Releasing All In Love And Trust.*

Being Right Is An Illusion, Let's Just Rock with Happy

Initially the chapter of this book was going to be aptly titled, "Am I Right and Happy", my intentions were to reveal and describe why it is wise to choose being happy over being right. Here's where the voyage in exploration of this chapter turned juicy. Being right is an ILLUSION, YES AN ILLUSION! Illusion is defined as *"a thing that is or is likely to be wrongly perceived or interpreted by the senses. A deceptive appearance or impression. A false idea or belief."* Here is where it gets personal for me and why my discovery was life changing, a complete paradigm shift.

For years, I, yes me, was on this strong kick about the word "should." I despised how I heard should used and implied within certain context. For example, I felt that "should" was used as a "you know better than that!" judgement and discipline tool. Author Louise L. Hay, in her book *You Can Heal Your Life*, sounds off well on the topic of "should". "I believe that should is one of the most damaging words in our language. Every time we use should, we are, in effect, saying wrong. Either we are wrong or we were wrong or we are going to be wrong." One last blockage that stood in the way for me with the "should" belief and approach, was hell, there "should" be world peace, no taxes, and free health care for all. Nevertheless, we as living, breathing souls and human beings have these mammoth variables that makes "should" obsolete.

With this being my illusion, at the time, I felt "right" or justified concerning my complaints and aggressive emotions when I heard people use the word "should". Let's fast forward to the present moment, where I have been enlightened in ways untold (I continue to be enlightened, never stop evolving, when you don't evolve, the side effects are tumultuous, possibly life threatening). While reading literature from one of my greatest teachers, Florence Scovel Shinn, guess what word she states needs to be a part of our intention, thought and belief process? Ding, ding, ding, "SHOULD"! I was floored, but **I THOUGHT I was "RIGHT" all this time.** Before moving along, I will share her "should," listen as you read her inspired pen: "*The divine idea for every man is plenty. Your barns should be full, and your cup should flow over*". Not only does "should" in this context set our feet and life on an abundant solid ground, it allows us to learn that "No, no, no, sweetie, what YOU think is RIGHT, could actually be the farthest from the truth", an illusion, as stated in the above definition. Before we press forward, let me inform you, of one of the causes, for our need to be "right". "*We tend to believe,* says Dan Mager, at PsychologyToday.com, *in the inherent accuracy of our thoughts, assuming our thoughts are facts.*"

Be clear, I am not speaking of instances where you have to take precautions or love someone from a distance. I am speaking of those husband/wife, friend/friend, mother/daughter moments where we have reached our ceiling of patience with certain situations and circumstances. To illustrate, we all have been on both sides of the coin. You know, we have cut someone off in traffic, been irritated by your companion's perpetual tardiness. The countless times where we have accidentally stepped on a foot or two and most certainly those grocery line wars. Yes, yes, yes! We can find ourselves "right" about many situations.

Here's where it gets ugly, "*the need to be seen as right is enemy #1 to love and marriage"*, WHOA! In addition to closing our hearts off from love (when doing this, you're a dead man/woman walking by the way)-our number one purpose for being here- physically you wreak havoc on your body. Reflect on the physical memories of your steam and bull-stance. Shifting your weight in fury (some of us to the point of a physical misunderstanding), attached with vicious, verbal lashings. Some lashings, causing erupting tears, foaming at the mouth, headaches, lastly, sore joints and fist from pounding whatever is available to pummel.

Guess what my amigos and amigas, in order to be right, you had to inflict "right" aka **PAIN** on **YOURSELF** FIRST. Who on earth is worth that level of mental and physical aggression? No, my love, yes, you are right, but the grocery store for example is going nowhere. Your destination is going nowhere. In fact, the soul that bestowed those actions upon you is probably world's away mentally, rendering them unworthy to drop your vibrations to a disappointing level.

What's That You Say?

What's the connection between releasing right and rocking with happy to weight release? Remember our friend Dan Mager? He states *"given the intimate and increasingly well-researched linkage between mind and body, psycho-spiritual imbalances have adverse impacts on physical status/functioning"*. Yes, baby, you want a neck turning, magazine-ready body, **LET BEING "RIGHT" GO!** "Right" pounds on your physical, storing itself as back fat as an example. Demands of being right, spreads itself to the pit and pendulum swing of your arms, and has the potential to turn your tummy into a flat out gut. Let my past photos serve as a physical testimony to being right. STOP! I could totally take several lines to place ourselves under a guillotine- there is no productivity in that! Yes, dear friends, being right leaks to our physical and creates expressions of our bodies that we would not otherwise select.

Moved to Drop a Moment of Silence

I'm feeling the pull to speak on comparisons. I'll explain. We all have those Phenomenon's in our lives (you may have been one yourself), who is able to consume just about anything. Case in point, the post-church buffet, you know, where you and the family would inhabit the space in an inappropriate manner. Mind you, growing up for me, the adults were equally engaged in our camaraderie. Yes, post-church buffets were swipe down both sides of the aisle –clean! It's there, those buffet's, that were totally created with Phenomenon's in mind. Here's why – Phenomenon's can eat it all (pause)!

Here's the makings of a Phenomena, and why they are labeled as such. Phenomenon's, those select loves of our lives, have the energetic ability to go "zero to one hundred real quick", the catch is, they are a size 4 or of some "accepted" physical caliber. One of my previous beliefs was "none of these stupid food and life rules applies to them, why me?" Oh, yes, I got you; that was me before identifying with my legal nature. Here's the point, recall as well as affirm the age-old adage "comparison is the thief of joy". Apply these words of wisdom to your soul, mind, body, and life. You are not Friend A or Loved One A, and they are not you. Release all notions of what you feel (or think) it is to be them, as well as how you feel you would act if you were them. None of that is real, NOR WILL IT EVER BE. Know and believe confidently your travels on this journey are specifically designed for YOU, you are a purpose by design in my Fred Hammond voice!

How to Release Comparisons

Man oh man, while the words Release comparisons may seamlessly roll off my tongue and on pen and paper, we all know actions are a different set of circumstances. Here's an antidote to cure a life-altering, bottom-barrel action, such as comparisons. You ready? We mind our own business! Plain and simple! Please raise your left hand (I'm left handed), and repeat after me, *"I mind my own business"*. Tending to our own affairs absorbs any need or desire to compare. Forming this mindset as a lifestyle both personally and professionally created wonders for my entire life.

Why do I need to mind my own business? When I focus solely on myself, I clearly see MY areas of growth. These areas apply to no one else but YOU and ME. Notice, it's YOU that shows up late regardless of the setting (ouch-back to that personal and professional). YOU angered by the slightest, troubled over any form of news, being relentless to others, which, by the way, is all an internal to external reaction. Minding our own business provides us with huge opportunities of growth. During this crucial period of development, we are able to observe those "splintered portions" of our soul. The beauty of this observation is that now we *Release All In Love And Trust*, and begin to take actions that suite the tide of our own universe instead of acting against those tides and flow.

Let's Face It

We can all read these words as life instructions on a page, but let's face it, application gets tricky at times. Creepy thoughts pop up and feelings of doubt and worry explode! However, recall, I said to AFFIRM "comparison is the thief of joy". An example of those creepy thoughts may sound something like, "Why did "Sally" receive ..." boldly cut that thought off and with confidence proclaim "I release all forms of comparisons against myself and others!" **Disclaimer: I receive affirmations all the time and tweak them to my liking. Do the same!

Let's Just Rock with Happy

Penning this bestseller (manifest) has brought me much happiness and joy. By the way, *joy is a surplus of happiness.* The articles I received from the Universe are amazing. To illustrate, Brian Vaszily's, "Being Happy-Experience 1 on How to Be Happy" article created the perfect definition of happiness to me. "Happiness is being right here, right now, and moving forward." I LOVE IT! Let's not stop here, we are provided with an excellent scenario to apply happy and weight release in our lives. "See and feel yourself tired or sad and believing you therefore deserve that giant hunk of coconut cream pie as medicine for your blues; then see yourself make the choice to bypass that temptation." Take a moment, right here, right now, and visualize yourself in this phase of the process. As a matter-of-fact, I will complete this rewarding, life-giving, baby step, with you. Right now, close your eyes, and visualize your strength, as you walk away, in love, from any form of temptation that is before you.

Just Do It, Be Happy!

Here's the invaluable lesson I learned. YOU, no one else, have to say to yourself "does being right - *eating endless slices of pie, extra cheese etc. over a long day or triggered emotion - make me happy - at peace mentally and spiritually, fitting in your jeans, achieving a particular goal*"? From experience, being right, invites temporary relief with long-term problems. **RIGHT IS AN ILLUSION! HAPPINESS IS EVER PRESENT** - Being right here, right now and moving forward. That's the right way to happy.

5 Ways to Burst onto the Happy Scene

1. Roll down a grassy hill
   (Please watch for traffic and critters)

2. Tell yourself (yes yourself) a knock-knock joke
   Knock, knock!
   Who's There?
   Lettuce
   Lettuce who?
   Lettuce in and you'll find out!

3. Tighten up your dance skills on the following moves:
   **Kid-n-Play
   (Foot must go completely over the leg)
   Cabbage Patch
   (Swing those arms in excellent circular motion)
   **Funky Chicken
   (A friend can join you on the Happy Scene)

4. Smile
   "It affects certain muscles that actually make you feel happy
   or joyful. Your brain sends even more happy signals, or
   endorphins."

5. Recall a Hilarious Moment in a Movie
   For me it's the movie Napoléon Dynamite, when Napoléon
   tells Uncle Rico to "get out of his life and shut-up!"

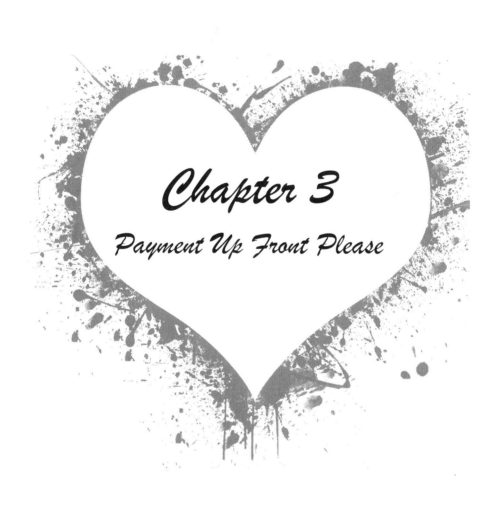

Chapter 3
Payment Up Front Please

Payment Up Front Please
Vibrational Match

In order for your Releasing journey to manifest through your physical (your body to Release weight), you need to know a few things, consider this your public service announcement. You are forever beautiful and fit, you just have to tune into your vibrational match. "Nothing rests; everything moves; everything vibrates". The third and last of the immutable Universal Laws, tells us that "the whole universe is but a vibration". Science has confirmed that everything in the Universe, including you, is pure energy vibrating at different frequencies". I explore vibrations later in the book, however I need you to set your mind now to who you already are, and that is "artistic gymnast" Dominique Dawes, or professional basketball players, Skylar Diggins-Smith, and Candace Parker, you take your pick, your soul will tell you your source.

Let's get into some good vibrations, and its importance. Often, we were raised or placed in a situation where we were not encouraged to be ourselves. Due to these events, our true likes and loves (vibration) became smothered. Not being able to accept and express your feelings good or bad caused us to have human reactions. The vibrations from those circumstances caused us to have mixed signals. Now that we are back on our feet and at home, we recognize our vibration for what it is, stunning, forever young, matchless and grateful. Here is why this stage and strategy is useful. Abraham Hicks, whom you should explore, breaks down vibrations for us powerfully. "You cannot receive vibrationally something that you are not a vibrational match to. So, bless those who are finding abundance. And in your blessing of them and their abundance, you will become abundant, too. But in your cursing of their abundance, you hold yourself apart from it. It is a law – it is a powerful law." This is crucial because our weight release is connected to our vibrations.

That's why any weight loss or get rich quick schemes dissolves before it fully gets started. "They don't change your behaviors, you can't expect to lose weight and keep it off if you don't permanently change your behavior". Guess what the key is to a change in behavior? You guessed it, your vibration. Maintain high vibrations by "focusing on learning healthy, lifelong practices such as portion control and eating only when you're physically hungry, that is when true change starts to occur."

Focus On Positive

While there are a list of things, that are easier said, than done, to sustain a true and high vibration, we have to focus on the positive. Over at RNCentral.com they leave you with some incredible tips to increase your vibration by focusing on the positive, I will give you 3 of their 100 Positive-Thinking Exercises, I selected these tips because words are also vibrational matches, they play a vital role in our victories.

1. "Only use positive words when talking. If you're constantly telling yourself "I can't" you may convince yourself that's the truth. Replace these negative words with positive ones instead. Tell yourself you will do your best or that you will try your hardest instead.

2. Push out all feelings that aren't positive. Don't let negative thoughts and feelings overwhelm you when you're feeling down.

Even if it's only for a few hours a day, push your negativity aside and only focus on the good things in your life. *Remember this one?

3. Use words that evoke strength and success. Try filling your thoughts with words that make you feel strong, happy and in control of your life. Make a concentrated effort to focus on these words rather than those that make you feel like you are failing or incompetent".

Universal Law & Order

"Everything in the Universe moves, vibrates and travels in circular patterns, the same principles of vibration in the physical world apply to our thoughts, feelings, desires and wills in the Etheric world. Each sound, thing, and even thought has its own vibrational frequency, unique unto itself". Yes, yes, yes, there is this crazy, yet truthful fact about the Universe, just like airplane tickets and arcade coins it requires payment up front.

What do I mean? For sure, you nor I would ever dream, let alone think that in 3-4 weight lifting sessions we would emerge with the arms of ageless beauty Angela Bassett. Never here on planet earth will that happen and trust me if it does, pretty soon you will be right back where you started. I didn't want to believe Oprah, declaring through my t.v. screen, when she would say "you have to put the work in". For me, that was the millions, now billions of dollars she earned, that was talking. Wrong! Oprah put her payment (Up Front) into the universe.

Let's make the connection between weight release and universal law

44

and order, think of a fad diet and why it's called a fad. "They mislead you," and you can't mislead the Universe. "You'll see the two little words that matter most –up to. That means that if you lose 1-2 pounds in 10 days, you're still a success in their book even though the picture they are trying to paint looks very different than the one they are actually selling you".

Setting a goal of Angela Bassett arms, is a wise solution. To get you set up for success with this mental and physical goal, in *11 Beginner Strength Training Tips for Women* you are encouraged to "stick to the basics. If you're just getting into strength training (or finally getting serious about it) you will be better off sticking with a few exercises for the first few months. Your body will remember/memorize a few movements much more quickly". Another tip I enjoyed and will employ is "using acceptable alternatives, if you don't have the mobility to deadlift a straight bar off the floor, you shouldn't dismiss deadlifting all together. You could try trap bar deadlifts, rack pulls, or even single leg deadlift variations". For all my male readers, C.T. Fletcher, has an ass from heaven, look up his workout regime. I will let you know up front that if you do check for C.T. expect to receive tough love, one of the slogans for his brand is "It's Still Your Muthafuckin Set", check him out, he is absolutely inspirational.

Universal Law & Order can allow us to receive our gift of weight release, and any heart's desire, we just have to be aware of our vibrations, and proceed in nothing less than the highest realms of possibilities. Please find the following advice a delight for your vibration and physical manifestation.

- "Find something beautiful and appreciate it.

- Beauty is all around us, yet so often we walk around with our blinkers on. Stop rushing for a moment and take the time to stand in the sun and appreciate your surroundings".

- Be conscious of the foods you eat.

- "Some foods vibrate at high frequencies, and some lower (broccoli has a high vibration as do blueberries; Big Macs don't vibrate at all). If you are consuming foods covered in chemicals and pesticides, or foods found within plastic packaging, it will leave you vibrating lower. Conversely, consume good quality organic produce, food as nature intended it, and feel the high vibrations disseminate throughout your body. Most importantly, *pay attention* to how eating certain foods make your body feel".

Payment Up Front Please Release Reminder

» You are forever beautiful and fit, you just have to tune into your vibrational match

» "You cannot receive vibrationally something that you are not a vibrational match to"

» Recognize our vibration for what it is, stunning, forever young, matchless and grateful

» "Use words that evoke strength and success"

» "Stick to the basics. If you're just getting into strength training (or finally getting serious about it) you will be better off sticking with a few exercises for the first few months. Your body will remember/memorize a few movements much more quickly".

Chapter 4

No Shortage Of Beauty

No Shortage of Beauty

Headed in one direction with this topic, the Universe quickly placed me on the proper path to express what I learned about this individual Release. No Shortage of Beauty was sparked from my prior belief in lack. In my heart and mind not only was beauty going to run out, there was a shortage of beauty as well. Guess what else? This shortage of beauty was also confined to a limited space and a limited group of people.

By now you've learned that I crave definitions and the discovery behind most of our daily rituals and sayings, so its only right that I provide the meaning of a word contributing to how I once lived my life – shortage. One definition of the word shortage exclaims "a state or situation in which something needed cannot be obtained in sufficient amounts". How icky, who feels warm inside about the fact that you take this definition and apply it to your heart and soul? To take a deeper measure for this Release, take a moment to consider what you feel is your heart and soul. For example, my mother, Sister Circle Friends, laughter, and my brother's dog Musa, who has been here before, are illustrations of my heart and soul.

To assist, attack and diminish our belief in shortages, a blog post titled "What Makes Something Beautiful" struck a cord within me. Here's why, what we deem as beautiful will inevitably consume large portions of our time. Therefore, its critical to investigate our true likes and dislikes. The beautiful "peace" to this search is that it will reveal what you believe is beautiful.

Here's where it gets tricky, we may consciously and subconsciously deem something as beautiful that is completely terrible for our soul. What do I mean? Consider the scents and cinnamon sweetness of a Cinnabon, how about the savory taste of fast Chinese food, sweet and sour aromas mixed with vegetables and deep-fried spring rolls on the side -go figure?! To be clear, nothing is wrong with munching down on the aforementioned foods, however overeating and lacking balance reveals a belief in shortages.

A belief in shortages within weight Release looks like but not limited to the following- "I must eat up, time is running out, I have to hurry and clear all the food on my plate and my sisters' plate should she not finish her chicken leg and side of mac and cheese". You know our shortage beliefs, "all the food, at least around me, is going away so I will just consume any and everything while I can". The other classic scenario, "I'm always rushing so I will scarf my food down at the same pace".

Let's move this shortage beyond food. What about the "man" in your life (psst, that's not a man, that is a boy), or your supposed friend who combined, the both, do not want to see you doing better than them. However due to the belief in a lack or shortage within our minds, naturally there is a shortage of friends and companions, so "I must squeeze and hold on tight to whatever type of energy I'm manifesting at the moment" – WRONG!!!! There is a major difference between being a help and being a hazard, when you are willing to clear up the shortages within yourself, the Universe will reveal who is playing what role in your life. To clear up our belief in shortages and lack, I have provided an affirmation from Flossie that has proven timeless for me and applicable across all of life's situations.

"The walls of lack and delay now crumble away, and I enter my Promise Land under grace".

"What Makes Something Beautiful" –The Beholder

To be clear, your Higher Power will not leave you stranded for information when it comes to the development of your soul. When you become willing to Release your shortage belief, the Universe will reveal what beauty means to you. Here's what's attractive about this revelation "beauty is in the eye of the beholder" and you dear goddess are the Beholder. When you begin to Release fear, feelings of shame and unworthiness, to give you an idea, you will realize there is no shortage of beauty – there never was, there never will be!

Here's why, beauty is what is believed by the beholder-YOU! Google.com defines beauty as "a combination of qualities, such as shape, color, or form, that pleases the aesthetic senses, especially the sight". The "aesthetic senses, especially the sight" is where we pay special attention. Here is where we can temporally accept as true, that there is a shortage of beauty, based on our false beliefs.

"The term aesthetics is defined as the perception, interpretation, and appreciation of beauty". To provide further meaning behind this characterization, "aesthetic emotions are experienced through vision, hearing, touch, taste, smell, and cognitive processing in response to respected stimuli. In the presence of beautiful things, we feel a broad range of emotions, such as fascination, awe, feelings of transcendence, wonder, and admiration."

Comparisons
The Thief of Joy

To express how we arrive at our beliefs in shortages of beauty, I combed through my healing process and received the common theme across my areas of growth. This thief of joy, which had me believing in small amounts of beauty, was comparisons. Yes, comparisons will snatch away a joyous life!

Back to definitions, I need to provide you with the meaning of the word comparison, as a matter-of-fact I will provide you with one meaning I found for the word compare. Here's why, words have power and words create our lives. Therefore, if I have an understanding of the general term of a word, I will treat my words like gold and currency that I possess. When my words exit my mouth, I over-stand that those words, require payment from my possessions.

Don't panic and be clear, we were perfectly trained and well-manicured to make comparisons with our lives and the lives of others. Post weight release I joke with my mother that I should have been mute until I was 35 years old.

Think of a perfect "comparison" picture painted and not an Augusta Savage or Romare Bearden. How about the pink elephant, tiger, and bear in the room that never gets addressed within our families?

We can create some very solid situations within our mind based on comparisons. The hot girl from high school, living an "All My Children" lifestyle in your mind, all based on comparisons in your life. How about when your bubble busted only to discover that you are a joy thief and a comparison whore, her story is NOTHING like the one YOU painted in your mind.

What about Beyonce, we completely leave out that she often has to practice with socks in heels, because blisters have formed on her feet from all that goes into her performances? No, comparison land, will have you totally focused on Beyonce's beauty, not the process that comes along with her beauty and success.

Oh comparisons, "he only likes her because she's skinny", hand raised, we are absorbed in comparison land, throwing out any facet of reality. Here are some items to consider when you take a moment to step out of comparison land and into truth. Is there a possibility the young lady or gentleman you are observing is sweet, are you? How about what draws your mind and soul to an individual, does Forever Couple A share common interests, bonding them beyond a physical attraction? However, the case presents itself, there is a young man or young lady that will actually check for you, Release your nasty habit of making low-vibrating comparisons.

Comparisons No More
Diamonds Are Forever

All right loosen your necktie and the anxiety that has flared with the recognition that you reside in comparisonville –that is the Release, so let us be clear on an even deeper level. While "Diamonds Are Forever", are you aware of a "century-old marketing campaign" that shaped a profound belief within our hearts?

Diamonds are actually an example, of one of the reasons we have a belief in shortages. What do I mean? Think of the reason you are searching for a ring to begin with, yes, you are either manifesting, or love has manifested on the physical plane and you are in search of the one item symbolic to represent your at long-last love – a diamond ring. While there is nothing wrong with a diamond ring or two, guess what, diamonds rings and romance, only collide because you are urged to buy more diamonds, nothing to do with love.

In an effort to increase brand sales, a company promoted the idea of a lack of diamonds, and what better way to tie in that shortage then by linking it with romance. A New York advertising agency, hired by the company in the late 1940's, promoted the "concept of eternity" through a diamond ring, yes, mere marketing. Through their promotion, they employed the idea that "a diamond that's forever promises endless romance and companionship."

My oh my, the fun to their promotion did not stop there, "newspapers would reinforce the link between diamonds and romance. Stories would stress the size of diamonds that celebrities presented to their loved ones, and photographs would conspicuously show the glittering stone on the hand of a well-known woman."

Who reading this text can say that a diamond ring was able to create a "circle of eternity"? Divorce rates and other callous actions prove that promotion fictitious. However, think of how we, as young ladies, are so tied up into a belief, that was created to take YOUR money, nothing to do with love or romance neither the juicy monogamous relationships and marriages that we yearn for as human beings, let's take a deep Release breath with that one!

Here is another reason why I felt "Diamonds Are Forever" was a perfect example as to why we have been conditioned to have a belief in shortages, I grew up in a very religious household and under the umbrella of religion wearing a diamond ring was tied up with someone's salvation. Meaning, if you wear this ring, hell is sure to follow in the afterlife, how terrible. You mean to tell me that through someone else's promotion, the Creator of me, you, and the Universe is saying that I can't join H/She in heaven over diamond rings, emeralds, and cubic zirconia's –Not So! Let's Release any form of beliefs in shortages, you are the hot girl and woman standing next to the equally hot girl and woman, we are all Queens! There is no shortage of beauty, its actually exploding and overflowing. Let's lean on and use an affirmation I learned from Dr. Michael Bernard Beckwith the first time I visited his Agape Feast - it's his church.

"Lord reveal to me, how beautiful I am, no matter how much it overwhelms me".

As a side note, I was not able to say this aloud during my visit to Agape, the tears poured and poured that day, however with a new belief and practice, I was eventually able to say it aloud and teach it to others. Please do not stop if a lump swells in your throat and you are not able to say it aloud for a while, as long as you push for it mentally it will come out physically and you will rejoice over what you once deemed impossible.

Wedding Dress Release

Want some wedding dress relief and Release? We are releasing all types of chains and bondages! Traditionally wedding dresses were actually crimson, yes, red, until February 1840 when Queen

Victoria, married her first cousin, yes, first cousin, Prince Albert of Saxe-Coburg and Gotha, breaking all forms of tradition by wearing white. "After their 19th-century reception, it became popular in Western cultures to wear a white wedding gown like the royal monarch, whose silk satin white design bucked the convention of wearing a red bridal dress for the big day".

Something interesting to note is that Queen Victoria was not the first royal to marry in white, however, she has been credited with the tradition becoming widespread.

Learning this powerful information was a mind blower to me, and well worth the research. This is why I stress reading and personal time; the Universe will rise up to meet you in ways untold. Information you never knew possible will explode onto the scene on your life, its o.k. if you are afraid, for damn sure I was, here is what you and I both must remember, if you are afraid or the dream is scaring you, then you are headed in the right direction.

Asian Eyelids
Trust Me There Are Distractions

Years ago when I was stuck in my belief in shortages, there was an award winning Asian journalist on a talk show where the episode focused on the forms of cultural beauty placed upon women. Here's why we have to Release our belief in shortages of beauty and know that beauty exist all around us. The journalist was a beautiful, well-traveled, professional that covered topics of meaning, so sure, her life was successful, and thoughts of imperfection never found there way to her mind and soul, not so. The young lady goes on to lament that within her culture to have a certain fold in their eyelids was considered a form of beauty, the belief is so widespread, surgery is available if you happen to be born without those proud natural folds. However, because we are all human, she goes on to speak about the torture she had to endure for not being born with those precious, perfect folds in her eyelids.

Let's say she never released her fears and clung to the eyelid belief, do you think she would have been able to tell that story years later, no? The belief was Released and the fears were faced so now she can sit on an internationally syndicated talk show and tell how she had to go through the process of releasing a stunted, inaccurate, belief in beauty.

Here is where we tie in weight release and a belief in shortages of beauty. Now as you may or may not know, to my knowledge I am not Asian however this is a true story and displays how deep of a well we can run within our souls. After the show aired, I found myself heading to the bathroom in panic, hell, I had to battle my weight and now I'm walking around without folds in my eyelids, what was next, I would become a teacher.

Upon reaching the restroom, I took hesitant steps toward the mirror, despite my furious quick steps heading to my destination; it did not take long for the inspection of folds in my eyelids to begin. Even then, the Lord was trying to reach my soul, during my examination I discovered that I was not Asian and that I very well may find myself without folds in my lids.

Folds or no folds, there is not a shortage of beauty, all that is you –

what you see in the mirror and after the shower - is beautiful! Let us reach for Lil Wayne when trying times are weighing down on our lives. "I don't think you're beautiful, I think you're beyond it"!

Trust me there are distractions, when there is a belief in shortages, you feel everything will be going away soon and you are going to miss out. Let me give you a clear example from my life. Prior to Releasing All In Love And Trust, I was a shopaholic, and my purchases ran the gamut, from clothes to home goods and wine, when I started generating a professional income, I begin to spend the way I was taught. Despite my income, the shortage pit I had to Release and climb out of was the desire for everything. Once, I was sipping on some guilty pleasure of reality TV. Having taken a rest from reality viewing, it wasn't 5 minutes into the show, and I revved up- where did she get that dress, her hair color is so on point, I want that look for summer, check out those earring, are they from Aldo's, where did she purchase her lip-gloss, I love its shine and luster? How about her phone and nail polish, by the way did she show what color under garments she was wearing because guess what, throw those in the bag as well –impossible!

Do I have Asian eyelids?

58

Yes my loves, when we believe in shortages everything has to go –
with us! No, we are not here to hoard and entirely consume, beauty
expresses itself in all forms and has no desire to stop being beautiful,
beauty is waiting for you to join in its expression.

Make You Free – Debrena

To bring this selection home, I want to gather a story from the
archives of my self-help journey. For years I consistently took all
types of spiritual and enrichment courses. As I look back, the courses
were of nutritional value, at that time, I was just not ready to hear the
joy and gladness these courses contained. When we speak on years
to becoming an overnight success, apply my self-help expeditions
here.

However, the time arrived, and I was ready to stop forking over
money and not totally consuming the benefits of what I was
purchasing. During one of my tele-courses the facilitator of the
course and my birthday sake Debrena made a statement that I never
heard in all my years of religious interaction. "The Son shall make
you free" with an emphasis on make.

In all my years of interacting with the saying and paraphrased bible
verse I was under the impression that it was set you free. Well here
goes, after all those years of self-neglect and on that call of 20 plus
releasing women, I spoke up and inquired about the difference
between set and make. It was then that the "me" you see now
awoke. Debrena goes on to explain, when something has to be set
free, its captive, like a gate that has to be opened to let you in or out.
From the foundations of your Higher Powers beginning, you and

I are made free, we are not bound by anyone nor anything, weight release, and shortages of beauty included. You don't have to be set free because you were made free!

Here's another confidence and esteem builder, after Debrena answered my question, a young lady in the group thanked me for asking because she was unaware of the difference as well, see how loving yourself first has a positive domino effect?!

Go Higher To Compare
You vs. You

Here's how we can develop our love of beauty and realize there are no shortages. For starters, we can take a deep breath because not all comparisons are unhealthy and low vibrating; there are positive comparisons that exist, and we can translate those comparisons into an accomplished goal.

For example, who here has attended your typical old Negro spiritual church service, where a young woman that ranges from the age of 65-92 years old, cries out how the Lord has bought her from a "mighty long way". Here's a healthy comparison, you vs. you, when I, Haven, think about where I was 3 short years ago, tears well in my eyes and I am visibly able to see the grace and mercy He has brought me through, that blessing and miracle runs internally as well as externally for my soul.

Another healthy comparison as a goal, would be connected to the HBCU where I received my bachelor's degree. During my days of training, there once reigned a superb first lady, I loved to deem her our university's Michelle Obama. Our first lady stood about 6 feet tall, educated, and carried her smile with her wherever she went. I was always in awe of her and rarely spoke to her due to my fears. However, with healing being a part of my make-up and genes, I no longer place our former first lady on a shelf in the fine china cabinet of my mind. Now I know in my heart that she is a representative and blueprint to what my life can and will be - a statuesque, spiritual, married being and woman, who expresses herself through her passion.

Beauty School Dropout
Go Back To School

Growing up I was an avid lover of musicals and still a fan of them today, the movie Grease was no exception and I would find a way to belt out those notes and dance moves somehow. In one of the films, a young lady was encouraged to return to school to get her like back on track, she was exploding with potential and a beauty school dropout that needed to go back to school.

To release our belief in a shortage of beauty, we have to do the same as the beauty school dropout and return to school. Be clear I am not speaking academia, however if you feel impressed to pursue formal training as a method of healing and progression you have my complete support.

Here is where we have to cut back on TV, turn our phones off to e-mail, social media and chit-chatting and open a book that will crack open your soul. Baby steps will always be the key, no matter the endeavor, let's start with reading 20 minutes daily, at least 3-4 times a week, this is necessary to open the layer of our soul that has to be accessed for healing and progression. As a former educator we always promoted reading for 20 minutes daily not only to increase your knowledge within your studies but for you to experience success in your life, on a long-term level. Trust me I am not trying to add another item to your list of life, there are incentives that come along with reading at least 20 minutes daily. You will find yourself empathic, with an expanded vocabulary, and your mental health actually becoming stronger and not facing decline. Get this, reading 20 minutes daily also has been linked to reducing stress, and we all know that stress can be one of the number one causes for weight gain. Implementing this strategy will prove beneficial in many ways weight release included.

Just think, if you took 20 minutes twice out of your day, one time for spiritual, the other 20 minutes to read about a hobby or side hustle you will find yourself moving through your ranks of belief much faster than you imagined, give it a try!

Beauty Sleep

While the beauty school dropout needs to return to school, she also needs to get some rest. "Years of research have revealed a strong connection between inadequate sleep and being overweight". There are so many factors that come into play in our daily lives sleep can take a back seat yet have disastrous effects.

We also need to pay close attention to our sleep patterns or lack thereof, society tells us that we need to work around the clock, despite being human and your body tearing away at the seams. There is an unspoken belief of "who are you to stop, keep going until you die"!

Here is one of the ultimate reasons that sleep needs to become a priority for successful weight release, "sleepy people tend to feel hungry and consume more energy than those who are well rested. When people are sleep deprived, their brains respond differently to unhealthy foods, and they are less likely to resist eating them".

There are so many different causes and factors as to how much nights rest you should be receiving. Take time to discover the actual amount of rest you need to achieve, based on your body type, so that you are able to experience successful, long-term weight release.

You vs. You

We know you are not the rich and famous or just rich – believe me, I would snarl when some form of media would express their vain gladness on how the latest celebrity was able to release their baby weight - which never seems to be over 20-30 lbs. max, in my opinion. Here's how we can mirror their actions instead of waving a white flag. If this particular celebrity was able to release their weight by doing 30 minutes of weight lifting daily, we can no longer get upset and say they are able to obtain their ideal body weight because they are rich and can work out whenever they want to-true.

We can ball and achieve on our level as well. What do I mean by this? You may not have 30 minutes daily to weightlift, how about 20 minutes, at least 3 times a week, hell since we are taking baby steps here, let us start with twice a week for at least 20 minutes completing some form of weight lifting or physical activity.

Along with this goal, make some time and space for mental exercises. Reading, devotion time, and speaking affirmations aloud to yourself, shifts your Universe, there is an element and energy so surreal, yet true, when you complete this step of the process. You will feel the joy of when you see your favorite celebrity, break down crying, when they meet their favorite celebrity, the tears will pour, you will do the stop, drop, and roll, lottery winner dance, the joy is overflowing and cannot be contained even if you attempted.

Here's what's foremost to this Release and I am speaking to myself as I am speaking to you. Embrace those tears and seriously lean into your dance moves, you never know the gift and promises that are WAITING for you on the other side. These words flowed through me because I am in the thickets of crying and showing vulnerability in the proper manner and direction. We cannot skip out on this slice of the process; your Release and gifts awaiting you are greater than the previous or temporary pain, you may be experiencing.

Let me take a moment to explain devotion time, it may have an intimidating sound however the benefits of devotion are endless, and this time, serves as a compass to lead your life. Growing up, my family had devotion, so I pull from those childhood experiences to direct my time. Devotion is like taking yourself on a romantic, intimate, date. Here is why devotion is crucial; devotion time is where you can receive the much-needed direction for your life and vent your frustrations to your Higher Power in an unfiltered way. Your Higher Power needs channels to express Himself through and S/He uses devotion time for you to listen to those directions. In addition to venting your frustrations during this time, you can also read a text from a spiritual or self-help author that creates devotional books. This is time well spent, in as much as possible create your own devotion time and space.

What Do You Consider Beautiful?

Considering the headline for this section of the book had me singing a couple of tunes that fit perfectly into my expression. For example, the now paired Christmas song "My Favorite Things" expresses what I consider beautiful. "Raindrops on roses, and whiskers on kittens, bright copper kettles and warm woolen mittens, brown paper packages tied up with strings, these are a few of my favorite things!" Cardi B's "I Like It", also expresses my sentiment. "I like those Balenciagas, the ones that look like socks, I like going to the jeweler, I put rocks all in my watch, I like texts from my exes when they want a second chance". Yessss!! When those songs end, I'm lured to Oprah's time of year, where she blessed those around her with her favorite things, oh the joy, remember the forever saying, "you get a car, and you get a car!" Yes, these are a few of my favorite beautiful things.

Yes, that's me and one of my besties pre-weight release and I still could not see my beauty
#nowigsnomakeupjustnatural

Here's why this is essential, if you never explore what's beautiful to you, you will never know who you are and realize the potential that is you. Before I move along, I wanted to leave you with my Top 10 List of Beautiful Favorite Things, remember, there is no right or wrong, the purpose of this list is for discovery and expression. Create your own and jot them down in your Release workbook.

Haven's Top 10 List of Beautiful Favorite Things

- **Vintage Photos of Beautiful Black Women** – there's nothing more beautiful to me than to see black women of old, donning their beauty through that time frame. These photos allow me to observe that there is nothing new under the sun and you have the strength of these beauties to grasp.

- **Wearing Ugg Boots Year-Round** – My mother and former co-workers love to hound me about this fact, yes, it's true, I wear Ugg's and Ugg type boots year-round and prefer comfort to my feet over the seasons. Hey maybe you enjoy wearing Ugg's or a derivative year-round as well, please tag me in your photos and hop online so that I can join in on your fashionista experience. Plus, I will get to show my mom that I am not the only one reaching for comfort year-round!

- **Pot-Bellied Pigs** – For years I have had an attachment to these animals despite their routines and sleeping arrangements. There is something about their soul that screams gentle. I often wonder if I am tying Charlotte's Web into my feelings however it's beautiful to me and has been my fave for a while.

- **Tattoos** –Tattoo's bear the human expression and allows a soul to paint or create art based on their experience, I liken tattoo's to storytelling and everyone you see and meet has a story, view their story one tattoo at a time.

- **Kim Porter** – Your beauty leaves me speechless!

- **Pure Comedy** – I love comedy in all forms, when you have a moment, please do yourself a favor and look-up 1940's Bad Invention Dog Restraint, that shit is as eerie as it is hilarious.

- **Fast Cars & Shooting Stars** – There's nothing like a fast and furious set of wheels to me! An all-black Ferrari is on my manifest list.

- **Jay-Z & Beyonce** – In real life they like goals! It Is So!!!!!!

- **Fashion** – Beautiful fabrics arouse and inspire me, there's nothing more cathartic then to explore fabrics and visualize a well-designed garment.

- **Shoes with the Proper Heel Length** – Now my idol Kimora, loves her heels at about 5 inches, cut that length in half for me. Not only am I cute and comfortable, when your heels get to high without the proper training, you will soon learn that it's a long way to the bottom in heels that high.

Your beautiful favorite things list isn't just about what you consider beautiful, it's about confidence building as well, you have to have the courage to love and be yourself first, why? Your list will reveal who you are, and some of those beautiful things that are you, may go against status quo, thus requiring you to stand up for your beliefs and heart's desire. Hell, sometimes it's not even the voices outside of you as it is the voice inside of you. Yes, this list is beautiful in more ways than one! Want another piece of motivation? Learning who you are, is one of the ways the Universe is able to rise up and meet you with its promises.

Please remember there are no shortages of beauty, and you are a part of that never-ending beauty. At this point the only thing left for you to do is celebrate and handle other business, your dream body is on its way! Below I leave you with some fresh reminders and affirmations from the chapter, I love you! Don't forget to hop online and in your workbooks to express what makes something beautiful to you and what are those beautiful things. Please reread this section should you have any questions about completing your own **Beautiful Favorite Things** list.

Shortages of Beauty Release Reminder

- Find your fave celeb body and tweak their routines to your life

- Please Remember your much-needed intimacy of devotion time

- We are all Beautiful, there is no need to dim another's light, remember Dr. Beckwith's affirmation – "Lord reveal to me how beautiful I am, no matter how much it overwhelms me!"

- To clear up our belief in shortages and lack, turn to Flossie's affirmation when you need to find a quick mental fix - "The walls of lack and delay now crumble away, and I enter my Promise Land, under grace".

- My mention of Chinese food earlier made me want to throw in some guidelines to remember when you enjoy Chinese dining. As a matter of fact, "Chinese food is one of America's most popular and healthy ethnic cuisines, but it can be high in sodium". Heart.org is exploding with tips across all fields.

Healthy eating, physical activity, and weight management are an example of the material they provide, the website is user friendly, please take a moment to browse!

» Skip the crispy fried noodles on the table"

» "Ask the cook to use less oil when preparing stir-fry and other dishes and to leave out soy sauce, MSG and salt"

» Steamed rice over fried rice

» "Sweet and sour sauce, plum or duck sauce" now or often replaces those heavy indulgences of "lobster, bean and soy sauce" *I always enjoy a little coffee with my cream, please keep me in your prayers on that one!

External Factors
View Yourself as A Business

To hit my target on external factors, I was able to locate two excellent resources to convey my message. Number one, view yourself as a business, yes baby, be a business-man! Yes, let's focus our weight release attention in the business lane. Here's why, if you view yourself as a business then you will learn not to take external factors personal. Reference.com points directly to what I mean when I say external factors. "In business, external factors are circumstances or situations outside the business that a business cannot control".

Placing an emphasis on "circumstances or situations outside the business that a business cannot control", external factors and weight release go hand-in-hand. "You must turn to external factors to effectively predict your future. There are a slew of factors to take into consideration that usually are beyond your control". In order to successfully attack our weight release on a long-term level and as a lifestyle, you have to become aware of external factors, and an external factor is anything outside of you! With that being said, how much control do you think that you have over anyone or anything aka an external factor? I'm going to Release and say absolutely none.

Place Value

As a teacher, one objective students learn is place value. Most of us have been taught the formula, there's a one's, ten's, hundreds, thousandths, place and so forth. Here's one of the goals of the lesson, you have to determine and know that every place has its own value and those values are not equal yet necessary. For example, there are issues in life that you wouldn't give a dime of your attention to, yet we can call off a list of things we desire to the tune of millions of dollars.

Let's even explore how you have to learn, that the number 5 in the ones place has a totally different meaning or value, if that same 5, was in the tens place. There is nothing wrong with the number 5, there is nothing wrong with the ones and tens place, they simple have separate meaning or value.

External factors and place value go hand-in-hand because you have to assign value to the things that are in your life. For example, you are cut off in traffic, it would be nice to express a case of road rage however that external factor has no place value in your life at all.

External Factor Smasher

Here's the thing, external factors are what we call life, and in order to get a hold of your life and not be swayed by external factors, you have to develop a sense of security. Now don't go collapsing, this security is not based on you or I, oh no, this security, is based on your Higher Power, and the Universe S/He had in place when you arrived, you know, your birthday. What I'm saying is, the faith you claim to have and believe on, you have to trust that it is working in your favor, and that those works are not based on your actions or anything you do. In order to deflate the value of insignificant external factors, "remember that this Infinite Power has never been defeated or frustrated by anything outside itself".

Response-able

No need to fear, Response-able is here! Throughout your Release and while on your journey through this book, you will learn, how big of a fan I am for online courses. I always recommend online courses and certifications to my loved one, here's the Release tip, online classes can work seamlessly with your schedule. Give at least one a try and let me know what you think and if the experience was worth the investment.

The online course I'm referencing here was one that I took on confidence, and yes, I recommend you locate several online courses and receive your Release confidence through several of those channels. In the first module on confidence I was directed to an aha term called "response-able", response-able is the perfect antidote for external factors.

Here's why, within the course, they go on to explain that response-able puts you in the driver seat of your life. Meaning, place value on the external factors around you, what is actually worth your time and attention? One way to determine the value of an external factor is to know where you are supposed to be. While this may generate a chuckle, I suffered from this ailment longer than I should have or desired.

Who here has a job, what about a spouse or a child, if you answered yes to one or more of the following questions, then your schedule is nipped in the bud, you know the priorities and obligations that come along with those roles, now you know where you need to be.

Let me link the two together, if you have a job, especially in the field of education, it is recommended that you either pick your work clothes out for the week on Sunday or at least the night before and in as much as possible pack your lunch. While this can be applied to many areas and occupations I'm coming from my experience because this was an area of weight release that kept my waistline expanded.

Rushing every morning to work, with an Oscar the Grouch attitude, there were no clothes picked out from the night before, where was I supposed to be? Ever the hungrier, I would swing by a convenient fast food restaurant where I spent money before even earning money, where was I supposed to be? Let's not forget what I'm chugging down my throat and system in the name of food, where was I supposed to be?

Lo and behold, there was a day where I picked out my clothes the night before, packed a lunch and even remembered to bring it to school with me. My waistline thanked me, the checkbook was fatter, my gas tank included, I had no need for unnecessary stops. My grouchy-rushy attitude did not find its way to me that morning, my oh my, knowing where I was supposed to be proved to be a powerful and universe shifting science.

Where I was supposed to be was picking out and ironing my clothes at least the night before, not talking on the phone or laying down. Where I was supposed to be was releasing low vibrating comments mentally and replacing them with what is real and that is "I am and I have". Determining where I was supposed to be proved to be key in turning my life around.

Trust me this is not a method or technique that I cling to with dear life and hold on to by the letter, this solution comes to mind when I have gone off track and want to holla out, why lord, when, I am not where I am supposed to be. We are all response-able. Here's also what happens when we fail to become response-able, our energy and power will be completely zapped. You see the phrase "a slew of factors" was used to describe external factors, imagine attempting to give your time and energy to a slew of factors, our lives our perfect evidence of those attempts, this written book is proof that my attempt at "a slew of factors" did not pan out.

Attitude
"The Longer I"

While in undergrad I had the awesome opportunity to be educated by a great, she is my mentor and a life-long educator, Dr. Bradley. During my days of undergrad, I did not practice being my highest self at all times and I thank the lord for the dedication and commitment of Dr. Jessie Godley-Bradley. Acknowledging our need to face society and the rambunctiousness of our class, Dr. Bradley supplied us with the poem Attitude by Chuck Swindoll. One day in class she had us focus solely on the first 3 words of the poem and they are "the longer I". Dr. Bradley's point to the lesson was that you, I, are in control of our attitude's, what is the state of your attitude? External factors exist however with your attitude in tact you become response-able.

Titling toward Seven External Factors of Business to guide the way, I will rely on most of the factors that attach to weight release, they provide the perfect example of external factors and how these factors play a heavy role in our lives and waistline.

Economy
Prepare For War In Times Of Peace

Money or lack thereof can surmount to loads of stress, with stress floating around our hearts and minds, we can become weary. Here's what you have to know, just as sure as there is ebb and flow in the ocean, so is the same for your life, you will experience the climb that it takes to get to the top of the mountain. This climb to the top of the mountain is not all bad, because you will gain the experience of compassion. The ingredient of compassion is always needed, compassion triggers love and opens the door for us to give ourselves a moment of human rest. With this rest and compassion in place you are able to proceed, with external factors in their proper place.

In addition to gaining the experience of compassion, the ebb and flow of life may leave you momentarily feeling as if you are the problem in your life and there is a defect within you –Not So! Everyone has to go through the process and no one is exempt. "The global economy is one of the biggest external factors that will, at some time, affect your business".

In the 23rd Psalm we are told that we will walk through a valley of shadow of death, however we have to lean on the other portion of this scripture that states "I will fear no evil for thou art with me". External factors, which are beyond are control, come and go, however when these externals hit our lives, we will acknowledge them for what they are, an external factor with no place value, we will fear no evil because our Higher Power is with us every step of the way. Breathe in this thought and know that it is true and real.

*Please remember your Higher Power is with you when you are in the pit of a battle, experiencing a mental rage session, or where you have more than enough proof to turn into Rambo. Dr. Joseph Murphy exclaims that when we say aloud or to ourselves internally "God is with me" this immediately destroys morbid thoughts. I have used this strategy time and time again and it never lets me down.

I do want to heavily note that when you begin this process and use your mental facilities to evolve sometimes it will take a moment for you to physically calm down, this is because you are human and there is absolutely nothing wrong with being human. You have to deliberately look at your hands and body to make sure that nothing on you is tense and that you are not physically replaying what you were mentally recounting. Once again, all of this takes practice however you are more than capable (able) to Release.

Finance

This concept was hard for me to accept, because at the end of the day, I treated my body the same way I did my finances, terrible. When I became a classroom educator, I did not have the proper knowledge on budgeting my finances and how your money is to be allocated. With a greater salary flowing in and at a steady rate, I applied all that I had not learned to my earnings. Here's where the self-hate got even worse for me, do you know that at one point in my career, I was working about 6 days a week and did not know how much money I truly earned, robbing Peter to pay Paul was no longer a dancing act, it became a routine.

Just when you think the fun stopped there, when I resigned from the classroom, do you think I adjusted my spending habits to reflect the money that was actually coming in-no, as a matter of fact this highlighted just how ill my spending habits were.

At the end of the day, I was shame and didn't want to deflate my ego and admit that I didn't know shit about spending and budgeting, given my age and educational background this made acceptance for me even harder, I would pummel myself mentally for not having a basic knowledge and understanding of money. Here's the beautiful Release, those habits are not permanent, once you become willing to let-go of certain beliefs and behaviors, you will discover resources, spoken in your language, that will assist you in advancing to the next level.

Be clear, when I say spoken in your language I'm not speaking of English, Spanish, and Arabic, what I'm stating is that when you begin to discover who you are and who you were meant to be, teachers from all walks of life will be on your path. You may select a book or YouTube video where you do not connect with the speaker or author, however you can go to the next book and video and instantaneously connect with the speaker and/or author. Search for teachers that speak your language, they are there.

Ultimately, place value and online courses allowed me to face my financial fears in a comforting manner. There are courses galore, on not just how to budget your personal finances, but all types of budget, from a business you own, to project management, you can acquire the much-needed knowledge of finances in a non-abrasive manner.

Weather
"That's Life Got To Learn How To Treat Her"

"Storms, tornadoes, hurricanes and wildfires are outside your purview of controllable business factors". External factors pop up all over the place, they don't just limit themselves to comfortable avenues that can be easily extinguished, no, trials will come, and there are events that you are unable to prepare for. That's life got to learn how to treat her. Be of good cheer, different seasons require different removal and shifting. Think of the times of year when it's time for summer to change into fall. Yes, there is major shifting, the leaves on most trees and landscaping say goodbye, and certain birds flock to warmer spots.

What about the clothes we wear? Our summer bunny attire is stored away and our nice fall boots, with infinity scarfs, adorn our frames, while we reach for the warmest in garments, yes, that's life you have to know how to treat her! Here's the beauty to all these external factors, your Higher Power has everything under complete control. There is a solution to your problem; this is just another example of walking through the valley of the shadow of death without fear because your Higher Power is with you.

Speaking of the fall, here is where weight release gets major, you have to know that as a human being your body responds to the seasons shifting as well, with the sun going down by 4:30 pm we can fall into some pretty slothful habits as well as experience some form of depression. "The truth is that for many people, the transition to fall is tough and the transition to winter is even tougher".

Several reasons for this is because we are "spending a lot more of the day in darkness. Research is increasingly uncovering ways that Daylight Savings Time affects physical and mental health. For everyone, it means more daytime darkness."

This is a season where we have to keep it moving, and this keep it moving does not have to be strenuous, just steady with our exercise routine. To note, this non-strenuous exercise, also includes how you are mentally speaking to yourself. You are throwing the blood, sweat, and tears, of your time and exercise down the drain, if you feel you are unable internally to achieve any form of success, weight Release included.

Please remember, this is also a time to step up your movement because we enjoy a robust of holidays that call for nothing more than snacking, eating, and drinking, oh buddy, we have to love ourselves and the fall season at the same time. Here's what I found to be marvelous in my life, finding balance with what you eat and making simple changes personally and professionally will begin to become extremely easy. You are healing and placing external factors in their proper place, this allows you to proceed mentally with 20/20 vision.

Infrastructure
"Mind Your Business"

"Changes in the local infrastructure may prove either disastrous or fortuitous to your company". When it comes to infrastructures, intricate pieces and planning, go into place for its completion, the same goes with us as humans. We are fearfully and wonderfully made, there are numerous master pieces which come together, that causes flow within our lives. In order to maintain the flow, integrity, and structure, of the building -which is you, you have to mind your own business.

Minding your own business, is as simple as avoiding gossip or shutting down the harsh voices in your head with a quick affirmation. When you mind your own business, not only do you reduce drama in your life, you can accomplish the goals impressed upon your heart. The same time we once used to chatter, or continually express, our gripes about a low-life, is the same time we have to mind our own business and get to our heart's desire.

An effective way to minding your own business would be to create and set a goal. Prior to my weight Release I use to believe that goals were frivolous and for supreme beings like Dr. Mae Jamison who accomplished her dream of becoming an astronaut. If there is a heart's desire pressing down on your soul, then you definitely need to create and set some goals. Even on a much lighter note, preparing for Monday on Sunday, for at least 3 weeks in a row, is a realistic goal to minding your own business. Here's why, when we get off track from our goals, confusion arises, why, because you are not minding your own business and dabbling in affairs that you were not placed here to handle. That's why you receive so much kickback and pushback from certain circumstances, it's the Universe's way of saying "mind your own business"!

Trends

Now that we are Releasing All In Love and Trust, we know that weight release is a lifestyle, the mental strategies we exhaust from now on, are for long-term use. "Fad diets can be very tempting when you have weight to lose (Release) and want it off yesterday. You get caught up in their gimmicks and hype, imagining yourself in a thin, svelte body, and, before you know it, you're entering your credit card information online, telling yourself that this is the last time you have to walk this path. All too soon though, you're right back where you began, and the cycle repeats itself".

Customer Base

Your customer base is entirely important, this is your foundation and support system. Who here has viewed a home, commercial real estate, or even a tree, who's base or foundation has shifted or crumbled? We are all able to see the lop-sided effects when a foundation, your customer base, lacks the proper support. External factors, such as those around you, play a major role in the success of your weight release.

It is a necessity to avoid negative people especially when you are re-conditioning your mind through weight release. "When you hang around negative people long enough, you pick up their negativity. When you listen to someone repeatedly say 'It can't be done' eventually you start believing them. So pick the right company!"

External, Internal Conflict

As an author I write across all genres, a genre I gravitate towards are mystery novels, with a twisted plot and murder attached, you know the good stuff. During my reading up on literary terms and the different techniques to tell a story, the term external conflict came to the surface. "External conflict is a struggle that takes place between the main character and some outside force". Here's where weight release and life come into play, this outside force or conflict can also be your internal voice, the voice that does not give you the best advice or will discourage you from pushing through to the other side of fear. There are several types of external conflicts, I'll reflect on the conflicts where we have to be a "laser-focused" main character.

"Character vs. Society"
Who Are You To Be.....

"This external conflict occurs when the main character stands up to support his beliefs and struggles against the social forces". This external conflict is captain to our Release because it's the external force that causes us to store our hate in food and low vibrating beliefs.

Prior to my weight release, I was hit with a comment often that left me as perplexed as I was angry. People from all walks of life would let it be known that I was "pretty for a big girl". While this comment also left me biting my tongue, when a designer created the slogan for a t-shirt, not only did I buy it in a crop top, I was relieved that this level of stupidity was being recognized for what it was completely idiotic! This is a prime example of how our self-esteem can be crushed time and time again.

Reflect on the flip side of the "pretty for a big girl" set-up, think on the times you expressed yourself through your style of dress or even found a garment that adorned your shape only to discover that not only are you pretty for a big girl, some are amazed that you can find beautiful clothes in your size. This conjures up a story of how my dad once told me that I looked good in some leggings despite my size. Here is why you acknowledge external factors and assign them their place value. Not only was my dad overweight himself and knew nothing of women's fashion, his lack of accomplishments in his world caused him to spew out feelings about himself. Coming from Don Miguel's Four Agreements, I had to learn not to take anything personal. "Nothing others do is because of you. What others say and do is a projection of their own reality, their own dream. When you are immune to the opinions and actions of others, you won't be the victim of needless suffering."

Character vs. Nature
"Don't Take the Storm Personal"

"In this type of external conflict, the protagonist struggles against the forces of nature, or an external environment". When you focus your life on evolving, you will begin to recognize circumstances that are beyond your control yet a part of the pilgrim's progress. Here's what to do, in a riveting Bishop TD Jakes sermon, Bishop goes on to explain how situations happen, they happen for a reason, because of this unchangeable clause, in life, "don't take the storm personal". "Thinking everything is 100 percent you fault -whether it's a failed relationship or accident- will affect the way you see yourself and the world around you. Mentally strong people take appropriate accountability. They recognize they're responsible for their choices, but they also acknowledge factors beyond their control like the state of the economy, the weather, and other people's choices".

In all of these circumstances and at one time or another we have reached for unhealthy thoughts and neglected mindful eating when an external conflict needs to be Released from our subconscious and environment. I will leave you with the following affirmation from Florence Scovel Shinn to surrender your low-vibrating beliefs when an external conflict arises in your life.

"I now smash and demolish by my spoken word every untrue record in my subconscious mind. They shall return to the dust-heap of their native nothingness, for they came from my own vain imaginings. I now make my perfect records through the Christ within – The records of Health, Wealth, Love and perfect self-Expression".

External Factor Release Reminder

» Place Value – assign place value to the external factors within your life

» Response-able – You are response-able to make wise decisions, check in with your attitude to ensure you remain in a response-able state

» Confidence – Confidence means faith, activate yours & "align yourself with those who build up your faith"

» Where Are You Supposed to Be – Create a calendar and schedule your week. Determine where you are supposed to be, particularly when messy moments appear, it's a possible sign that you are not where you need to be

Chapter 5

Have Structure, Release Timelines

Have Structure, Release Timelines!

Fellow Releasers, I need your attention for a moment, actually this stop here is a non-negotiable. Establishing structure is the foundation of our weight release. Tossing to and fro within your life, demonstrates the constant see-saw thoughts and beliefs in your mind. With this being the consistent forecast of our lives, we do not stop to make healthy food selections.

Here's why this is important to know, you could be placing loads of anger and hate on yourself, and blaming your obesity on generational curses, not that it is not a factor, however your food choices are a reflection of your life. Meaning there's chaos in your life because you are chaotic.

The consistent seesaw thoughts and beliefs I spoke of, notes a life of indecision. This right here was an ouch for me. I was able to observe, how being indecisive is costly, and not just pertaining to weight release. This observation gave me the motivation I needed to build my confidence and Release any and all feelings of unworthiness.

Florence Scovel Shinn, one of my favorite Truth Teachers, also notes how being indecisive creates a tumbling block effect within our lives and how our health is punished from indecision. Ladies, we need to listen up because that even applies to hair-do's, outfits, and shoes. 30 minutes on what to wear, with matching eye shadow, for 1 outfit to go to the grocery store, let's Release this level of indecision. While I am seriously joking, what it boils down to is TRUSTING YOUR JUDGEMENT! Please remember Releasers, this strategy and advice applies to all areas of your life. TRUST YOUR JUDGEMENT!

The reason we create structure within our lives is because we are developing long-term, lifestyle weight release, nothing about Releasing All In Love and Trust is a quick fix or fad. This is now how we proceed with our lives, on a daily basis, not just in spirit but in truth.

Structure Me To Lifestyle

While you may not initially believe that lack of structure has led to your numbers on the scale, let me have you take a second glance at your behaviors. 10 Ways To Know You Need Structure In Your Life must have observed mines, to know what to write about. For example, one of the ten ways had me pegged! "You have no deadlines to get important things done. If you have no real shape to time, the illusion of time will take over your life. We have to shape time to create things. You need to start from a deadline and work backward, setting dates that you actually have to keep". Releasers, consider the times you set a date to begin working out or eating healthy only to fall within the lines of the quote above? My hand is raised. Let's even think on professional goals you may have set, yet your lack of structure did not allow for completion.

The author even called me out on a behavior that I long ago needed to Release. "You talk a lot and do very little. Don't talk about it, be about it. If you want to make yourself feel better about doing nothing by talking about all the things you are going to do, you are doing yourself a great disservice. You need to do the things you need to do. Talk about them when they are done!" You read the introduction to my book, how long ago was I supposed to finish this book and create other hot text for you to read? Yes, lacking structure has multiple side effects that read like medical prescription commercials.

Before I move on as to why timelines have to be released, there was also another lack of structure in the article that my friends and family have always teased me about, and that was sleeping. Taking naps after school transitioned into taking naps after work for me, yes, it was that bad. Guess what? This is also a sign of lacking and needing structure. "Your sleep cycle is a total blur. Blur meaning: I sleep when I want to, and I am awake when I feel like it. Try waking up at the same time every day. An early time will instantly help you to restructure yourself. When you are on a chaotic sleep schedule, according to Traditional Chinese Medicine your organs get confused in their own cycle. You may feel less effective because you are less effective!"

Timelines No More

Triggered through a conversation with a dear friend, her venting allowed me to examine my beliefs as well, here's why, she sounded just like me with her grievances. The same emotions flared as myself, her tone of voice accented certain words and expressions the same as me, so what was the problem, why were we both experiencing crash and burns within our lives despite effort.

Creating unrealistic expectations through timelines is one of the ways that we promptly arrived at crash and burn. Here is what I mean and an example of what we do, "by June... I want the body of, for the month of May I am going to run a mile, in the morning, daily". This step is the one that kills us the most. When we create unrealistic timelines, and not achieve our goals, we are murdering our self-esteem. Here is why we feel so bad, have you ever been told a promise that was not kept, how did that make you feel? If your feelings felt like drinking pickled pig feet juice, then ding, ding, ding, you are right on the head. Well guess what, you are somebody, and you told you that you were going to achieve a certain goal by a certain time. It was a promise that was not kept, even if it was you that said it. Your self-esteem takes a plunge because once again you have been let down, and this time you have been let down by yourself.

Now that we are releasing unrealistic timelines, we need to remember "to start from a deadline and work backward, setting dates that you actually have to keep", this is one way that we can keep from letting ourselves down.

Release Me To Structure

As I bring this piece to a close, I do not want to tell you what you "need" to do and not provide a strategy and solution. "The answer lies in carefully designing a routine that works best for each of us, one which helps us be productive, in control, and be the best person we can possibly be". At the beginning of this chapter, I mentioned that I would be brief so I will leave you with two of the best solutions I researched in order to build and maintain structure within your life -the foundation of your weight release.

The first to make my list is one that I feel creates a successful day, which leads to a successful life. Ever since I became laser focused with my self-help journey, I often experience the benefits of starting the day on the right mental foot. "Stick to an intentional morning routine. Routines create consistency in our schedules, help with time management, and encourage us to build healthy habits". Be determined to start your day correct, here to, is where you will have to practice self-love because you may have some quirky morning routines, be willing to love yourself enough in the morning through those odd behaviors. No need to fear, I have some quirkiness to myself as well, it's about honoring those feelings in the proper manner and space.

The last solution ties into my feelings of self-love. Here is why this is major, for majority of our lives we were taught to love ourselves last or barely at all. "Make time for self-care. Once you've planned out your week with appointments and to-dos, its vital that you plan some downtime to recoup. Take a look at your schedule and pencil in your favorite self-care activities or time to do absolutely nothing". Releasers these self-care activities do not have to cost money, the library, coffee houses for conversations and relaxation, and walking the neighborhood are all cost effective, healthy, self-love activities. Do not feel that extravagance through cash always has to be the solution.

Examples of Life Structures

"Exercise classes are life structures that help maintain wellness.

Hiring a weekly housekeeper is a life structure that can eliminate mess, and A weekly menu plan is a life structure that can help you maintain a healthy diet.

Head over to your Release workbook, and jot down 3 simple ways you can create structure in your life. Please use the examples given as a tool, to help you set realistic goals for success.

Release Me To Structure Reminder

»   "We have to shape time to create things"

»   "A weekly menu plan is a life structure that can help you maintain a healthy diet"

»   Creating unrealistic expectations through timelines is one of the ways that we promptly arrived at crash and burn

»   "Start from a deadline and work backward, setting dates that you actually have to keep"

Reach out to me through social media and let me know what structure you had to put in place to get your weight release ball rolling!

High Vibrations = High Confidence

"It is my dominant intent to feel good!!" This is the affirmation the Universe sent to me while I was indulging in my addiction of Instagram. In an effort to clear my thoughts and gain an understanding of how our thoughts arrive, I would click on the IG accounts of different earth angels and read their various post. During one of my daily ventures, I discovered this ever-helpful affirmation. Here's what makes this saying juicy, the moment you place this phrase out into the Universe, "doors open for you, people flock to you, money flows to you! Vitality oozes from you, charisma is you!" There are even moments where I will replace the word good with excellent, boldly proclaiming, "it is my dominant intent to feel excellent!" Please take this affirmation and tweak it to your soul's rhythm and flow.

Often times our thoughts can become quite impulsive, and flat out grotesque. With this being the case, we must become guarded with our thoughts. When we become guarded with our thoughts we will begin to achieve a higher vibration. "Once I understood that the universe is immaterial – it is mental and spiritual, and the entire material world is nothing but vibration – I understood the importance of keeping my own vibrational levels high". Wait there is more, there are perks and incentives to maintaining a high vibration, "when you have the right vibration you supercharge your ability to manifest". Way to go! Now that we have developed an understanding, there is a purpose to maintaining a high vibration, - that's where your heart's desire resides.

To release weight binding beliefs and external factors you have to have high confidence in yourself. The key to high confidence is a high vibration. What is a high vibration? A "vibration is simply the movement of our energy through space. Our vibrations are very important because they are responsible for how our lives unfold". Trust me Releasers, there are so many simple indulgences that we partake in that lower our vibration.

I'll place myself of the truth block first. An example of a behavior that kept me from a high vibration, was when I would take in salacious amounts of reality t.v., I didn't just take in reality television, World Star Hip Hop and YouTube would find me taking in vibrations that scraped the bottom of the barrel. "Many shows on TV are violent dramas that focus on the real world. On top of that, there are commercials that have you thinking you need pills to fix your problems and that you have to buy expensive jewelry to show someone you love them". To be clear, I respect all hustle however I needed to reduce my intake of "reality" that was not of a higher vibration.

What Is A Vibration?

Oh, you may still ask, what is a vibration? I am going to break down a vibration in Releasing layman's term. All that is you, is a vibration! From your beautiful, elegant eyelashes, finely shaped hips and thighs, and a navel that reflects your personality, that is a vibration. How about those chiseled features and that strong chest, how does this strong chest allow you to stand? Let's not forget about your ever-cool personality and distinctive laugh, oh a vibration is all that is YOU! Don't worry, there's no need to duck away from a vibration, you can't escape a vibration if you wanted to, a vibration is you.

A knowledge of the presence of vibrations, allows you to know how to carry yourself despite the life circumstances surrounding you. "Low vibrations provide signals to us that our thinking and behaviors are headed in a direction we don't want to go, and these signals can be very useful if we are aware of them". In order to recognize the awesome traits within you, you have to be keenly aware of your vibration.

Vibration On 100 Trillion
No Lack

The desire to obtain a high vibration may trigger feelings of inadequacy, you may believe you are incapable of achieving this state, however, Release that fear, it's a sign of low self-esteem and there is no longer a need or space for devaluing behavior. Here's why you don't beat yourself up for your previous responses to different low-vibrating acts. We've had a lot of false starts, for example you, like me, could have had a toxic childhood or was being held down by your own polluted beliefs.

At the end of the day, we all have faced some form of a circumstance that caused us to withdraw any feelings of a higher vibration. Meaning we have been in situations that has either destroyed our confidence or we had to call upon our confidence and it not being available at that time. Here's the fun part, and why its everything to research and learn for yourself. Confidence means the one thing we only need a mustard seed of, that is -faith, yes, the word confidence comes from the bloodline of faith.

In order to achieve high levels of faith, you need to secure a relationship with your Higher Power. "There is no real security apart from your sense of oneness with God". Here's the thing, if you are fighting or holding back from your heart's desire, not only are you fighting the God in you, you are saying no to your Higher Power as well. You don't hold back, because, despite your fear, your potential is waiting to explode and it's looking for pockets and places in your life to express itself. From the explosive acts in our lives, to the gentle pulls of your soul, "there is an urge within each of us that cries out for union with an Eternal Source". Check in with your faith, that is how you will find your Eternal Source!

If you happen to find your faith a little crumbly, be of good cheer, your baseline has been established, and you are aware of where you need to begin. Here's why it's worth doing a check-in, why would you believe lowly for yourself and others? These feelings signal a belief in lack, there is no lack. The late, great, Dr. Wayne Dyer states "you fail to project into the world what you fail to see inside". If I'm unable to see good in "Billy Bob" that means I am unable to see good within me? Yes! That's why you must check your faith and determine what you believe. You will immediately begin to identify and destroy all false thoughts.

Weapons & Ways

Your faith and confidence may be waning, because you are looking in the wrong area. That's correct, an abundance of lack can also be an indication, you may not be in your lane and looking in the wrong area. In order to Release this belief in lack, here is where a career and personality test is recommended, these tests serve as a guidepost to point you in the direction of your heart's desire.

Here is how you boost, prune, and shape your confidence. You "have weapons and ways ye know not of", the choice is yours to take ahold to the possibilities that are yours daily and by the moment. What we must know(ledge) is that "God works in mysterious ways, His wonders to perform." The weapon and ways I speak of may be called your subconscious, the God in you, that internal voice. Weapons and ways are the promises you must tap into for His wonder to be performed within your life.

Here is where we, as humans, go wrong, "the trouble with most people is that they want to know the way and the channels beforehand. They want to tell Supreme Intelligence just how their prayers should be answered".

Flat out, no way around it, in order to gain the high vibrations needed for high confidence we have to "have the expectancy of a little child and your prayers will be answered". This strategy isn't tax bracket or age friendly, when you pray, or express how you want a heart's desire fulfilled, you have to place yourself in a mode like "a child waits with joyful expectancy for their toys at Christmas". Yes, you have to have the faith, to the extent of, how you believe, that after Sunday, comes Monday. "Your part is to be a good receiver, prepare for your blessing, rejoice, and give thanks and it will come to pass", mental and physical weight release included.

Keep It Bouncy
Secret Sauce

Keep it bouncy, is a secret sauce that I unearthed post weight release, not that keeping it bouncy wasn't in existence, the layers of low vibrations within me, held me back from acknowledging it's presence. In order to access the weapons and ways we all carry, you have to add my spread of secret sauce, over the plate of your life.

To "keep it bouncy" is not your family member's ill-mispronunciation of Beyonce. "Keep it bouncy" means to "look for the positive in past situations and future events". For years I didn't partake in my own secret sauce, and it caused me to kill off my confidence and shut myself off from having streams of fun -better known as living my life.

Here is what a bouncy person does, although there may be places in their life that is not to their satisfaction, they still sing their favorite song, maintain a positive attitude, and go with the flow. When the daily developments of our character are being tested, a bouncy person remains calm and handles a given situation in balance. Here is where we head back to faith in our Higher Power and being ever the more cognizant of external factors.

Here are a few strategies and activities that will help you achieve and maintain your "bouncy" attitude and personality. Have you ever taken the moment to listen to the soul of an indie artist through their lyrics? What about neo-soul, have you taken a dive into a dimensional experience that will leave you yearning for more? Placing yourself in such a setting will definitely keep you bouncy.

Be clear I'm not speaking of front row seats at Madison Square or VIP tickets to the next concert, I'm speaking of creating a concert through the speakers of your phone, laptop and headset.

Trying times do not pick the perfect setting to upsurge, therefore a given situation may not allow you to listen to a song at that moment, however because we all poses weapons and ways we know not of, you can always play melodies in your mind. 10 Practical Ways To Raise Your Positive Vibrations agrees that proper music is a perfect tool to raise your vibration. "If you want to attract love, listen to songs about real, passionate, long-lasting love. If you want peace, listen to music about peace and relaxation". Now, while I did highlight the positive side of music, the article also informs us that "lyrics of hate, pain, violence, drama and fear send messages to your subconscious", speaking of those weapons and ways, remember how I stated that that is what I call my subconscious? Things that make you go hmmm! Releasers lets be ever the more attune that we are listening to the appropriate music to access our higher vibrations.

Another gift of "keeping it bouncy", is that it helps you "avoid temptation." This plays a connection with weight release, because "there is growing research that those who are more successful in achieving their goals don't actually have better willpower. They're better at avoiding temptation all together". Meaning, this doesn't just include food, low-vibrating people and situations are a temptation as well.

Reminiscence on the experiences and wild times you gained, while out with your friends. What about the much, talked about undergrad hot spot? Where you and your crew discovered that the atmosphere at the club, was not worth the entrance fee nor the outfit you graced everyone with. Events like this, always guided my first steps to the bar, to satisfy this mishap. Yes, having a drink because you are bored or upset is very real and an avenue through which we can fall in to temptation.

Fly Girl
Omar Tyree

Omar Tyree's best-selling novel *Fly Girl* sits in my heart and top 5 books like Mildred D. Taylor's Road To Memphis, I had the excellent opportunity to meet the author, at a women's empowerment event years ago. The joy to express to Mr. Tyree that his book played a pivotal role in my life was priceless. Let me tell you what else was priceless, his genuine, red-self, asked me what my other favorites books are, after that, you know I am a permanent Omar Tyree fan. Actually, you can't go wrong with most of his books, so pry one or all of them open.

With no intention of giving the details of the book away, Tracy Ellison, the books main character, was a fly-girl, in my heart, I aspired to be her, yet had no courage whatsoever to display or live out her acts. In my opinion *Fly Girl*, innately, was equipped with everything that I desired to be. "Tracy is beautiful, intelligent, and armed with self-esteem and a sassy mouth". Who was your neighborhood fly girl, did she make you think of Nia Long or Jada Pinkett-Smith?

Here is where Fly Girl meets our healing and weight release, Tracy's life reflects the fly-girls we already are, should we choose to access our weapons and ways. Yes, fly-girl's still experience a wide range of emotions, yet she,like Tracy, presses through anyhow. Here's why you need to do the same, especially if you want to tap into YOUR fly-girl status quickly. "The higher the frequency of your energy or vibration, the lighter you feel in your physical, emotional, and mental bodies. You have little, if any, discomfort or pain in your physical body, and your emotions are easily dealt with. You manifest what you desire with ease".

Here's the valuable lesson I learned post weight release, the barking, snickering, and laughter I use to pour on a fly-girl's routine, from hygiene, to their rare social media interactions, is what you must do, whether you are single, married, or dating. In addition to their hygiene routine, and mastery of mystique, if you also want some fly-girl action, it will not appear, if you are still stuck in morbid beliefs. "The lower your vibration, the more likely you are to attract circumstances to you that mirror this and the higher your vibration the better you attract, and doors open to all the positive stuff!"

Trust Me, If I Knew Then!
Miami 2001
#TheLordkeptmecovered #AleeshaDKnew

The hardest part of the Fly Girl lesson for me is maintaining that flawless appearance. We all know that one fly chick that stayed around the way with the latest outfit, manicured nails, lashes on point, matching shoes and a purse to complete their look, it seemed as if chick never had an off day. Unfortunately for me I previously had more off days than on and I allowed my "I don't care" defensive attitude fester in my appearance. My first year of teaching elementary, I had the opportunity to work with an excellent 3rd grade team. When I wrapped up my first year of teaching, my teammates presented me with a gift I have to this day and it was a scrapbook over my first year. Man oh man, those darlings had to scrap together some pics for that book, however they pulled it off in a superb manner. It wasn't until I viewed the pages of How To Be An Overnight Success that I learned the prime reason to maintain that fly-girl appearance. You are your personal brand, a reflection of all that is you. "If you are just starting out or in the early years of development, YOU are the brand. You need to always put your best foot forward to make a good impression for your brand".

Are You A Hot Girl?
Supporting Cast Member

We've covered the outside, let's focus on the inside. Now that you are fly, let's Release you to fly and hot! Yes, a Releaser, is fly on the outside and hot on the inside. When we begin to walk in who we truly are, which is are heart's desire, you will begin to take hold and mold what counts in your world.

Here's step one in hot girl success, you have to be a supporting cast member. This may sound odd and contrary to popular belief and practices however, we have to know, when it is our turn in life, and when we must be supportive. "While the lead actors in a movie are extremely important, if they don't have a good supporting cast then the production will fall apart".

Here's the other beautiful Release, now that we take our power back, we get to select our cast members and who we will be supporting. Meaning you may be the best supporting actress or actor, yet you have joined a cast of trash, and receive trash kickback. There are no victims, there are no saviors, which is why you must wisely select your troupe.

The Release and forgiveness peace for yourself and others is, when you lack self-love, you can make some lackluster choices until that self-love has been gained. How about falling in love with yourself first then selecting a cast you know is already supportive, i.e. a fly, hot, girl or boy, man, or woman. When we have selected our troupe out of self-love, then we, ourselves, are Releasing and preventing the production of our lives falling apart.

Be clear, I am not stating that in your life you are a supporting cast member only, I am stating that one of the roles you play has to be supportive. Here's why, "supporting characters, are often key sources of revelation in the story, unmasking aspects of personality, motivation and backstory that might otherwise have remained hidden. They can remind us why the journey of the main character is important, especially when that character is most troubled or lost".

Here's why it's ever the more important to be a supporting cast member, my dear, this is life and you will have your turn at the spotlight. You will need a supporting cast, if you are alive, you are not "an island, peninsula maybe" however you will need assistance. Who are you going to be able to run to if you have not established yourself as a supporting cast member? This is why it's worth the investment of being a supporting cast member. When we treat others the way we want to be treated, we open ourselves up to a world of love, that especially embraces us when hard times temporarily press down on our lives.

A Place To Hide
Be Pippen Not Jordan

"I ain't got to shoot, I got mad assist" is a line from Nicki Minaj, that explains what it means to be a supporting cast member. In life you are going to want and need someone to stand quietly with you, show support in silence. Be clear this silence does not mean that you are still, it means be Pippen, not Jordan. "Pippen was the ultimate supporting player, the perfect complement."

When Pippen and Jordan worked together they were cohesive, that does not mean that they did not disagree, Pippen knew when it was time to think, speak, and act. In order for the team or your life to be successful you have to remain the "perfect complement". Pushing your agenda and speaking because you can, will cause you to elude becoming a cast member that receives callbacks versus kickbacks.

Why Am I Talking & What Am I Thinking

A step in the direction of becoming a supporting cast member is to apply what I mentioned previously and learned from Hay House author Gabrielle Bernstein, it's the W.A.I.T. acronym, why am I talking, to be able to answer this question, you have to ask yourself what am I thinking? "Every single thought that comes into your head has an impact on you. When you change those thoughts and think positive, happy, sparkly, thoughts, they become things too". Its here that you have to use integrity to answer both of those questions, it's here that you will discover your intentions and become responsible for your actions. Often times we feel "inspired" or lie and say it was from God and offer up a piece of advice that could have stayed where it was. We must be keenly aware of the words that are leaving our mouths. Here's another reason to be keenly aware of the words that are leaving your mouth, those are the words that you could be speaking over your life. All is not lost, and we were just in the wrong direction in the conversation department. This is a planet that is exploding with countless worlds, there are far greater words to be expressing, then placing low vibrations on our lives and the lives of others. I'll end with this, please keep quiet, silence is golden, apply it to your life -you are here to be a supporting cast member.

Just to shed some light on how it's a benefit to be Pippen, or a supporting cast member, there are multiple perks to being a hot girl, "in some cases, especially in ongoing material such as comic books and television series, supporting characters themselves may become main characters in a spin-off if they are sufficiently popular with fans". Yes, when you play Pippen, you win as well, where was Pippen when Jordan collected all his rings? Pippen was right there beside him celebrating and collecting rings to! Here's another Pippen fact before I let go, "Pippen only failed to make it to the play-offs once, in 2004. Before that, he appeared in the play-offs sixteen times in a row". Yes, be a Pippen, so you can gracefully have your turn at Jordan!

How To Remain A Pippen

It's not all peaches and roses being a Pippen, you yourself will have to tidy up your "messy" behaviors and take an honest approach as to who you have allowed in your circle. This revelation will reveal some mind-blowing information. You may learn that members of your circle may not be the best for you. Here's why this is important, "you can raise your own energy levels by hanging out with people who vibrate highly. Choose to surround yourself with people who are empowering, have the same morals as you, and see how much you rock".

Selecting a high vibrational cast is a must in order to maintain and remain in Pippen status, your whole crew, your environment, determines your success, and you are in control of your success, select your cast wisely.

How To Achieve A High Vibration
Yep! Happiness Is A Choice!

"You combine with what you vibrate to, so let us all now vibrate to success, happiness and abundance". At the end of the day, yep, happiness is a choice. This is a wise choice because it causes a smoother life and brings forth what we actually want out of life. In order to achieve this happiness we will hop on our vibrations. I will wrap this section up with different ways to achieve a high vibration. In your Release workbook, write down activities that help you achieve a higher vibration. Begin building a list of activities, as a reference you can look to when times get tough and sticky. Please hop online and let me know some of your favorite "happiness is a choice" doings, you might have a "happiness is a choice" technique that I am able to adopt.

Kicking off the list, and what has been my biggest Release, is being ever the more aware of my thoughts, remember the other W.A.I.T. acronym, what am I thinking, well place this here. To make the connection between weight release and what we are thinking, in *Why Falling Off the Wagon Isn't Fatal,* you are warned against belittling yourself. "For starters, don't berate yourself for being weak. Instead, tell yourself, 'I made a mistake. What can I do differently next time?" After that, you **MUST** shut the lion's den door to that past situation.

Next, be "excited to wake up and start your day". Here is where we stop and acknowledge what will be. Yes, there are days, times, and weeks where your to-do list is overflowing. It's in these particular spaces and places, where we have to tread lightly with ourselves and others and make it our dominant intent to be happy and grateful. Believe you me, there were days when I arose and the mental rage within my mind awakened before me. When we get to thinking about what has to be done for the day, gratitude may begin to take a backseat. This is the key, "courage and endurance are part of the system". We have to start our day on an excellent foot, this is our life, and we deserve the best that life has to offer. One way to make it through the day, is to "go with the flow! A high vibration will keep you in an optimal state of productivity, flowing easily from one movement to the next. You will feel perfectly balanced, neither overwhelmed nor bored."

Now that we have cleared out the mental trash talk and are grateful to start our day by going with the flow of our lives, let's make a mention of a space that dominates our life. That space is our home, "walls have ears and respond to the vibrational energy of the owner of a home". Prior to my weight release and dive into self-help, I did not realize how major your very own words and environment shaped your life -even if these sayings or words, are wall art in fun or a simple joke. It wasn't until I read a text by Catherine Ponder, that I was able to grasp how deep these simple objects and colloquiums create death within our lives. Ponder explains the depth of having ill pictures and sayings displayed throughout your home and business. All those pictures and sayings gracing your wall, are actually an invitation for those energies to appear.

Yes, we no longer invite the negative, however the opposite is still true, adorning your space with words of peace, abundance, and manifestation, will turn your home into a haven. Lean towards "flowers, warmth, fresh, clean, uplifting décor and colors", coming home to a place that washes away the day, assist you in maintaining a high vibration.

Behavior Mod Techniques

Now this may sound silly however this is how we go wrong in unwanted situations and circumstances. We apologize to ourselves and the other party, and truly express remorse, however, when its time again, we still reach for the same behavior despite the collisions caused by our actions. Behavior, often times, has caused us to dig ourselves in some deep ditches. Instead, there is a SOBER acronym we can all apply to our lives, this helps "deal with a slip or fight off the urge to do so.

- S – Stop – Pause for a moment and consider what you are doing

- O – Observe – Think about what you are sensing, feeling and experiencing and what events led to the situation

- B- Breathe – Take a few deep breaths

- E – Expand – Your awareness and remind yourself of what will happen if you keep repeating the unwanted behavior and how you will feel afterward

- R – Respond Mindfully – Remember that you have a choice, that you are not powerless, and that you don't have to continue the undesired behavior"

Last but not least, watch a comedy, you never know the cathartic favors a comedy will pay you especially during moments of ill, I watch Napoleon Dynamite all the time, no scene gets tired to me, and I'm elated that the cast of characters still intrigue me almost a decade and a half later.

List of Positive Higher Vibration Words

To get you on your way, I compiled a list of words that we speak to attract what we want in our lives. These therapeutic words are also used to calm us down during moments when our peace is being disturbed. Go ahead and write some of your favorite words down in your Release workbook. These same words and more can be written on some card stock or index cards to carry with you throughout the day. Life will happen! ⊡

Ability	Acceptance	In Balance
Authenticity	Awareness	Beneficence
Bliss	Cleanliness	Consciousness
Salve	Courage	Creativity
Decisiveness	Elegance	Endurance
Energized	Enhancement	Enterprising
Exaltation	Intelligence	Laughter
Love of Life	Love of Men	Love of Women
Loyalty	Luminous	Luxury
Majesty	Manifesting	Mediation
Miracles	Nourished	Nurtured
Openness	Poise	Productivity
Source-Light	Love In All Its Forms	

Self-Forgiveness		Self-Preservation
Simplicity	Soul-Salve	Succinct
Thrive	Tranquility	Transcendence
Trustworthiness	Upbeat	Vibrant
Vitality	Wholeness	Wholesome
Willing	Wisdom	Worth
Worthiness	Wow	Zeal

High Vibrations = High Confidence Release Reminder

» "It is my dominant intent to feel good!!" This is the affirmation we use to start the day and when our vibrations are being tried.

» There is a purpose to maintaining a high vibration, you are able to achieve your heart's desire.

» Always remain a supporting cast member

» Please Remember: W.A.I.T. - Why Am I Talking & What Am I Thinking

» Be Pippen Not Jordan - In order for the team or your life to be successful you have to remain the "perfect complement".

*#Shesthe**Scott**iePippenforme*

Vibration Release Poem

By Haven Turner

What Is A Vibration?

Oh, you may ask, what is a vibration?

I am going to break down a vibration in Releasing term.

All that is YOU, is a vibration!

From your beautiful, elegant eyelashes,

Finely shaped hips and thighs,

And a navel that reflects your personality.

Oh, you may ask, what is a vibration?

Those chiseled features

And that strong chest,

How does this chest allow you to stand?

Throw it in and let's not forget

Your ever-cool personality and distinctive laugh,

Oh a vibration is all that is YOU!

Don't worry,

There's no need to duck away

You can't escape a vibration if you wanted to,

a vibration is YOU!

Cry Over Spilled Milk
In Food And In Life

"Let's look at this mental preparation from a new angle." While that is a line from the book, Beyond Booked Solid by Michael Port, we must shift our paradigm to grasp this point of view. First let's explore the meaning behind the widely used term "cry over spilled milk". Cambridge English Dictionary defines cry over spilled milk as "to express regret about something that has already happened or cannot be changed." First and foremost, CRY IF YOU WANT TO, now we love ourselves above all else and acknowledge those moments in our lives where we need to cry, especially if it "has already happened or cannot be changed." Cry over spilled milk in food and in life. When you ponder on things that can't be changed like death, sure you are to cry and express anger. Releasers, death – the "cannot be changed" is what pushed me to completion of this book. You don't think I shed Kim Porter tears? Oh yes baby! Cry, cry, cry, you are human, and yes, in life, some things can't be changed. Let's bring this point even closer to home for you and me. Replace that spilled milk with marriage or relationship(s) that have been Released from our lives. Consider weight release, career expectations etc. you can fill in your own "milk" blank. If it spills naturally you will cry, it's something you wanted, thought you needed and definitely craved.

It Happened
Now Scream!!!

Who here enjoys the fall? The fall is my favorite season. Ponder all that takes place within nature for a season to change. During certain seasons, your award-winning grass will not reflect it's scheduled, glossy, sheen, appearance, however, you might be pretty mad if during the warmer seasons, a variable interfered with you entering the "King of Subdivision Landscaping" contest.

How about a few more, you, by hand, wash and wax your car and it rains, and not just a drizzle? Speaking of rain, what about being fresh from the salon? Yes, Releasers, we can spill milk from the simple to complex.

The problems arise, because we were taught to compress ourselves, into these unrealistic dehumanizing molds. As if, "don't you dare have a human response to something you hoped for!" All of those dehumanizing molds are a resounding "NO"! Please remember if someone tells you otherwise, those are not your people, run as if you are Sanya Richards-Ross. You must take a moment to acknowledge your emotions, even if they are low-vibrating, a season has changed, this shows you are human and growing, now we express our heart's feelings and emotions. We no longer need to be shelled and shelved, It Happened Now Scream!!! Cry over the spilled milk you yearned for.

There Was A Purpose For Your Milk
Acceptance

Acceptance for Haven became very real through my forgiveness work. Forgiveness and acceptance go hand in hand in my life. Here's what I learned, that acceptance, like forgiveness, does not mean that you agree with the circumstances, it means you acknowledge it's presence-it happened! Here's why you say aloud, and cry if you have to "it happened, I'm not the first, what are the solutions".

115

Acceptance also means that you are saying its time to let go of the pain. You declare to your soul, mind, body, and Universe that you are exhausted from hurt and anger's song and dance. You feel this desire burning even further when you are observing individuals both young and old thriving and exploring life. "It is vital you learn to live life on life's terms if you want to develop emotional sobriety"- what I call acceptance. "Living life on life's terms doesn't mean you give up on trying to improve your future – *it just means you accept what is already here because this can't be changed.*"

This Is A Planet For Crying Out Loud

Quick Release Reminder: This is a planet, long in existence, prior to our mere visit to this space, get out and explore, with acceptance comes options, do not limit yourself or your Holy One.

He Loves Me, He Loves Me Not
What Your Failure of Acceptance Births

While acceptance is easier said and read, when proper attention is not given to a situation, our failure of acceptance births some harsh realities. Prime example, once again, was my lack of acceptance within my life, thus birthing this book. I failed to accept my body for what it was, accept my mother and father for who they were, failed to accept my study habits were non-existent, and well we all can fill in our previous failures of acceptance. A "Stanford University study on emotions revealed that individuals with a tendency to repress their feelings reacted with a much greater physiological activation in trigger situations than others who, for example, showed anxiety or anger. For this reason, it's also normal for those individuals who don't express their feelings or who have much more difficulty doing so to have more somatic problems such as muscular tension, headaches, skin reactions, or complicated illnesses. Their emotions find ways to be channeled in less functional ways."

This was me, all day, every day, and be absolutely clear, all those "less functional" reactions I experienced were not due to me being a teacher, there was a failure of acceptance on my part. The consistent pace of life will bring forth the areas in which we fail to accept. Here's why, long before I was educating in the classroom I suffered from hellacious allergies, headaches (like my Big Momma), insane Charlie horses and the ever so present raging bitchdom. While the students may be out of control and public education questionable here is an example as to where I did not practice acceptance.

Here's Why Acceptance Is Dope
"The Practice Of Acceptance Is Enduringly Difficult"

Here's the deal, as you continue to grow and heal your views will totally shift because you are becoming aware of your true self. Your needs and desires will also take on this shift because you are no longer in a certain space. View that shift as beautiful, I liken this experience to moving into a new home especially if it's an upgrade or heart's desire. You don't get upset that you have to hire movers or pack your belongings with your crew. No, you are elated that your heart's desire has finally come true. Yes, moving is arduous and may cause a loss of a friendship or two however you had your eyes on the prize and grabbed it. So, it is with acceptance, "the practice of acceptance is enduringly difficult" however acceptance goes down all the time within your life, it's applying that same acceptance to the icky spaces of our life that are crying out for you to not avoid them. "Learning acceptance is a lifelong process, and we're guaranteed to be given plenty of opportunities to practice."

"Acceptance Is Not"

"Giving up your needs
Ignoring or denying a situation
Never asserting your thoughts/feelings
Acceptance does not equal agreement"

Cry Baby
Unhealthy Ways We Cry Over Spilled Milk

Where were you when Johnny Depp's timeless face graced the silver screen for the 1990 motion picture Cry Baby? Although I am Forever 21, I was about in the fourth grade, so 9 or 10, when Wade Walker appeared in my life. Regardless of my age, I instantly connected with the characters on the screen and wanted to be a part of their enticing gang. To show you how deep of a well that ran for my crush for him and the movie, I still have a Johnny Depp, Cry Baby, mug shot t-shirt, post weight Release. With all the full-figured clothing I sold, I just couldn't let Johnny "Wade Walker" Depp go! But shhh, tell him I said so!

Here's where the movie fades away and we are no longer crying due to injustices and the biased beliefs and actions of others. Here is where we turn into that whiny cry baby, you know, your cousin's toddler, that is beyond time out. Yes, that type of cry baby, except we all have some decades under our belt to be this type of cry baby.

Trust me our cry baby tears run deep, oh how deep you ask?

Let's begin here because here is where I need to raise my hand, and one of my main reasons for penning this book-overeating. This term may conjure up some unwanted feelings, but that's swell, it lets yourself and The Universe know that you are truly ready to Release this behavior. Here's the forgiveness "peace" for you and myself, "if you're overeating, there's a valid reason. Approaching these reasons and the overeating itself with curiosity and compassion-rather than moral judgement- creates the space, rest, and room to respond to your needs differently and to grow out of overeating." Hallelujah-the highest form of praise! While in the past we may have found ourselves overeating, there is a way out and it does not require us to tote around a customized guillotine. *Before I move along, I want to quickly highlight the beautiful vocabulary our overeating solution brought forth, words such as curiosity, compassion, grow out of, rest, and room, ooh la, la! None of these words are harsh, yet they are therapeutic and freeing - therein lies a mental strategy with a physical solution aka those lb's will be Released and your scale will note the difference. *Make sure that when you are in the throes of overeating or a sticky situation to slowly back out mentally with kind and noble words to yourself, you deserve this love first.

The fun does not stop there with our cry-baby behavior, how about that daily commuter traffic to work, where you and about how many other people are headed to their place of business? Yet, because you are a cry baby, they cut you off in traffic on purpose, and are on their cell phone chit chatting, because he or she knew that you would be right there at that same exact time. Above all, you never in life have done that right? How about those perpetual long-line stores, you know, the one where whenever you head in its packed? So congested are the lines, the person seated next to you at the basketball game, whom you have never laid eyes on and rooting for the other team, quickly agrees with you, that this same store has the longest lines as well. Yet cry baby you and me will most certainly believe that all those customers chose to purposely (don't forget) go to the store at that time and hop in line in front of you.

Side Note: If you feel that any of those statements are true and The Universe pulled your number, please reread this section. While I am being humorous if you feel everyone is coming for you, even after the stranger who stepped on your toe apologized, dear cry baby, we must reexamine our beliefs and Release.

Grab You Some Ibuprofen
Gratitude You Know

While acceptance is the order of the day, you will need particular tools to assist you on your acceptance journey. An impressive, research-based piece on gratitude pulls me in the direction of how I am going to round out this section.

Gratitude-liken it to Ibuprofen, were one of Ibuprofen's known attributes is to reduce inflammation amongst other medical needs. Here's the salve, we can easily attest that when some milk has spilled in our lives it can ignite internal and external inflammation. Gratitude is our "profen" as the old folks use to say to reduce and Release this type of inflammation. I'll let you in on 2 of the 37-research backed "benefits of gratitude" that resonated with me as oppose to unacceptance. Check out the remaining 35, you may find another "benefit of gratitude" you instantly connect with, which will also be a goal in reading the article, for you to find your personal benefit of gratitude.

While the benefits of gratitude are endless one that caught my eye was number 5- "It reduces envy. Psychologists say that gratitude is one of the best ways to reduce envy. It does this by reducing the amount of social comparison that we can sometimes do." This benefit stuck out for me because how often does envy creep up our spines and into our thoughts, more often than we would like for it to happen. My women Releasers ponder the list of comparisons we make based on a rubric society created. Here is another space where I can get personal and it rings true to home, I was considering a Brazilian butt lift and gathered photos of what I thought were women's real backside. No dice, it took less than 3 minutes for my best friend to tear through those photos and let me in on a secret, those weren't natural asses I selected, they just found a doctor before me. To be honest, I was actually jarred because I considered myself one that is able to pick out falsies however my selection of "natural asses" proved to be a photo of 1, yes 1! Oh lord, grab some gratitude cause envy and comparisons are actually fake.

The best one to me was #7, "gratitude boosts your willpower – the more you regularly experience gratitude, the more self-control you have in various areas of your life." We all can wave our hands in the air, especially in the name of weight release where we have to practice self-control on all levels. Not just from pushing back from the table in moderation, but the self-control and willpower to follow through with going to the gym or taking that Zumba class, how about your goal of not spending and eating out for the week (God this truth is painful)? Yes, grab gratitude, because willpower is needed for the journey and completion.

Cry Your Eyes Out
Healthy Ways To Cry Over Spilled Milk

For my female Releasers, remember, girls just want to have fun and are made of sugar and spice and everything (kinda) nice. With that said, create your own list of just wanting to have fun. For example, I was given horseback riding lessons as a birthday present one year, I also love to browse luscious magazines to manifest my future and best-selling designs. Nothing gets me salivating more than a selection of Hearst magazines- let me preface and label this activity as addiction territory.

Speaking of birthday presents and healthy ways to cry over spilled milk, one year while I was teaching, I took a yoga class for my birthday. I promise you the mental peace I experienced felt like I was physically walking on clouds. Here's the gift I extend to you, take a 1-time yoga class, its calming, gentle, and non-resistant. As we progress through the stages of life we will undoubtably face hectic moments, a call to your center for peace is a much-needed tool. My idol, Kimora Lee, (don't you say nothing bad about Kimora) has yoga as "The Ultimate Stress-Buster" in her book Fabulosity. Under Law #13 Strive For Fabalance section, Kimora expresses how she is "a calmer and happier" person once she has taken a yoga class and how she was not head over heels for yoga despite her husband's ultimate yoga dedication. "When I bend and twist and sweat the frustration and fears out, I'm much less quick to jump to angry reactions afterward. The nastiness of the world doesn't poke and prick at me so much because my stress level goes down." Notice despite being a successful, multi-millionaire and married (at that time) to a bon-a-fide wealthy man, Kimora expressed how she experiences fears and frustrations, my lovely Releasers, this is all the more reason to cry over spilled milk-this is truly a tax bracket aside situation here!

Before I move on, I want to add that just because I attended that 1-time yoga class, that does not mean I became an instant yogi. No, it's a process with learning how to fall in love with yourself and yourself first. Please do not begin to believe that anywhere from 5-6 days a week I'm in someone's hot studio stretching it out, no, 5-6 times a year is generous, however with Releasing All In Love and Trust that frequency is sure to increase.

I'm Singing In The Rain
"He Ain't Shit"

Another lens to view this Release through would be through entertainer Eve's role of "Terri" in the Barber Shop series. In an effort to elevate and Release old, stale, beliefs, and behaviors, "Terri" takes an outdoor class where she learns different poses and stretches to cope with the throws of daily life. Here's where this applies to you and I, Eve's character does a ka-rah-tay (karate) ish "He Ain't Shit" move with her classmates – this move isn't just for the character Eve played, this move applies to you and I. When it comes to icky thoughts and emotions, demons of the past long gone, you have to break out your "He Aint Shit" ka-rah-tay move or moves, its ok to develop a few. Self-sabotaging thoughts and situations emerge in the game of life, fight back with the proper energy and tone-whip yourself up a personal ka-rah-tay move. PLEASE DON'T ALLOW ANYONE TO TELL YOU WHAT YOUR MOVES NEED TO BE!

"A Moment Of Clarity"

I need to grant a moment of clarity, I am not just male bashing here, if you need to change that he to a she go right ahead, replace it with whomever-your boss, neighbor, siblings, the list of Releases can run long, so let's stop with the examples here.

Create Your Own "He Ain't"
Let's Get Physical

To begin, your "He Ain't Shit" move does not have to be a rough sport or Laila Ali boxing moves, my goal here is for you to create a physical Release to cry over spilt milk. Notice I took yoga? Please Remember, Flossie likens the Release of these emotions to releasing "Walls of Jericho", we have incredible emotions that require crafty ways to be Released. Secondly, note that you do not have to make a big commitment to a yoga studio or uber hot girl, never big-boned, gym. Instead, head to your local YMCA, community center or community college to receive that best bang for your buck and time. Another cost-effective method to consider, would be to check out sites like Groupon for a personal trainer looking to get their brand off the ground and in the atmosphere, thus creating an opportunity to receive their services at a reasonable discount.

I Need Someone To Scream
Here's How To Cry Over Spilled Milk

- Cry (Of course)

- Scream

- Paint Your Nails (Hell I purchased a nail artist course on Groupon, $5-true story)

- Breathe

- Google an article as to why you are encouraged to drink a glass of wine a day, then have a few sips-of course in moderation and consider merlot. ⊡

- Listen: Future & Lil Uzi Vert – Too Much Sauce – There goes your hype man song to get you back on your feet!

Healthy Ways Release Reminder
End of Chapter Wrap Up

» Create your own "He/She/Situation Ain't Shit" physical move that works for you. FYI-Since this is a physical Release I wouldn't choose just any setting to release certain frustrations, Dave Chappelle's "When Keeping It Real Goes Wrong" was more than just a skit to some, dare I say even more. Yes, I do crack myself up!

» Please Remember – check in mentally to ensure that you are not toting around an internal customized guillotine, QUICKLY GRAB SOME GRATITUDE.

*Another side note to my Johnny Depp romance, I purchased 21 Jump Street on DVD due to my never-ending crush.

* Quick Tidbit From Me To You

Chapter 6

A Peace Of Cake

A Peace of Cake & A Piece of Cake

Marvelous things begin to take place when you begin your Release. Oh yes, my loves, you can have a piece of cake and a peace of cake! When the salve was placed on my eyes, of where true healing lies, self-love changed my habits. A piece of cake, red velvet, my fave, became that, a peace of cake. This peace allowed me to not over indulge in not just cake, but any food, meal, or emotions.

The icing on the cake to this Release is, you can truly have and eat what you want. This is why I feel programs like Weight Watchers is so successful because yes, you can have what you would like. Now that we are Releasing All In Love And Trust, we lean towards healthy, and rock with portion control. Here's something valuable I had to learn, we are not being told information concerning our health as a way to pound down on each other, instead we have to listen up, there is a solution to these seeming epidemics.

I am not saying this to be mean, your stomach is only a certain size, your heart can only bear so much, your arteries and kidneys can only consume a certain level of intake. It's not necessarily "no, no, no, you cannot have, I'm being the mean, wicked, witch", we were not designed, nor shaped to over eat. That is not portion control, as we slide into this section, let's define portion and let's define control.

One definition of portion that I located was "a part of a whole, an amount, section, or a piece of something". O.k. Releasers let's look back at the first part of that definition. A part of a whole, let's go with, a whole pizza, now that we implement portion, we know that while there is a whole pizza, we only consume a part of a whole, a portion. There is nothing wrong with pizza, should it get consumed all the time, I'd fall back and place a limit, however when we look at the definition of portion, it's simply a part of a whole. Not that you can't have pizza, you just need a -portion.

Witnessing my Mom's successful weight release, I was able to capture and create my own journey from her experience. It was here that I discovered, yes, you can eat anything you like, just in control. O.k. the word control, let's focus on that definition. Another location defined control as "the power to restrain something, especially one's own emotions or actions". Oh man, this knocks us right back to portion, let's say, while there may be a whole pizza available for me, a whole box of Krispy Kreme donuts -ouch for me Haven, a whole pot of greens, a whole turkey, we must exert control. Be clear, once again, there's nothing wrong with greens and turkey, the only thing we are going to do Releasers is remain in control. Here's one of the reasons why, the "smorgasbord effect" is alive, real, and for the taking. "Having to many choices at once can lead to overconsumption because foods with different flavors and sensory qualities whet the appetite, even if you are physically satiated –the smorgasbord effect, this is why there is always room for dessert". Oh, room for dessert, before I get there, let's not drink our calories as well. The author of the article How Liquid Calories Can Sabotage Weight-Loss Success adds "even more of a culprit is sugary mixes for cocktails and frozen drinks". Yes ladies, when we indulge in happy hour and get in our Essence fest mode, those discounted drinks we partake of is like having entrée after entrée. Might I add, don't let the table talk be delightful, the entrees, I mean drinks, continue to flow. Think about how many entrees through drinks we actually have, ouch and yikes!

Now that we are on our way learning about portion control, a humorous, yet true story rises to the surface of my mind. This story and once a practice, must be told, because when my family and I graced the place of this restaurant, our control went out the door which meant so did our portion sizes. Decades ago, there used to be a family favorite restaurant called Healthy Habits, NOTHING was healthy about our habits. Our portion sizes were outrageous, and hell, not going to lie, we even took shit home, nothing healthy about that familial habit. Here is where our dear friend and companion portion control comes into play, while the restaurant may have served healthy items, they may have even provided us with the proper size bowls and plates however trip after trip, cookie after cookie, there was no control over our portions. We completely ignored the boundaries of the plates, pasta spilled from our bowls topped with the "healthy" sauces, yes, while they may have been providing healthy habits we did not apply portion control to any habit.

I would like to insert a question that you may feel is not connected to weight release. Since all events in our life are connected you will soon learn the relevance. The question for all you Releasers is –do you have trouble saying no? This is not a form of tough love either, my finger isn't wagging, badgering you saying, "did you say no at the bar, and pull back, did you say no to grandma's bar-b-que chicken?", those are not the no's I'm speaking of, are you able to say no outside of food? Here's why this is worth the search, you may be beating yourself up for not saying no to food because you can't say no within your life. "It's a simple fact that you can never be productive if you take on too may commitments – you simply spread yourself too thin and will not be able to get anything done, at least not well or on time". In order to approach portion control in a healthy long-term manner, we have to approach portion control outside of food. Here is my peace of advice to you, a tip, from a piece titled The Gentle Art of Saying No, "stop being nice, it's important to be polite, but being nice by saying yes all the time only hurts you. When you make it easy for people to grab your time (or money), they will continue to do it. But if you erect a wall, they will look for easier targets". Releaser's start saying no outside of food and best believe you will experience saying no through portion control with food.

Set-Up For Success

Let's set ourselves up for success, we are going to accomplish our weight release goals by moving forward despite any obstacles. There is a vivid and connected picture between our personal and professional lives and we choose success for both, we now know that we are worthy to receive. The first thing that I, Haven need to do and consistently be aware of is cleaning out my kitchen, I have to be honest, this clean out is in more ways than one, hell, I'm Releasing with you. "Toss out high-calorie, high-fat, sugary foods that will tempt you to overeat – chips, cookies, crackers, ice cream, candy bars, and the like. Then, fill your fridge with lean protein, fruits, vegetables, whole grains, nuts, and good fats". Yes, my loves and Releasers, we were not setting ourselves up for success by stocking our fridges with unhealthy food. I have to remain keenly aware of this because at times I have become slack with my food choices now that I have released a significant amount of weight. Be aware just because you are slender or not overweight, that does not equal to healthy, you can truly be unhealthy on a slender frame and think that you are cheating the system, you are not!

"Variety is key", although we Release the smorgasbord effect, we still want to open our palate to all that is available. Please release the notion that just because you can't have a fried hamburger every other day smothered in your auntie's family sauce, that you have to do away with the sauce or hamburger. There are tasty, nutrient, foods that exist and have been around for centuries. Since portion control is the major topic at hand, let's take a moment to explore some examples of what portion control looks like!

What does a healthy serving look like, "an ounce of meat or cheese is about the same as the size of your thumb from base to tip. Three ounces of meat, fish, or poultry (a normal serving) is about the size of your palm". Another portion control strategy that I have used was eating my meals "on a salad plate, instead of a large dinner plate". Once I attended a restaurant with my friends and discovered 2 benefits to portion control, one economic, the other waistline. "When ordering out, share your entrée with a friend" that's exactly what I did, I received a thank you from my pockets and satisfaction from my tummy, mission portion control accomplished! Although restaurants have cut back on this one in recent times, "ask for a kid's meal or small size at a fast-food restaurant, never go for a supersized portion". Please remember, the strategies that we are adapting here are for a lifestyle of long-term weight release.

Here's a cool researched fact, so that we can cease throwing daggers at ourselves for not being able to practice portion control. "Food servings have grown larger and larger over the years and fast food restaurants aren't the only places you'll find supersized meals. Researchers have noted that from 1970 through the 1990s, portion sizes of hamburgers, burritos, tacos, French fries, sodas, ice cream, pie, cookies and salty snacks increased, whether the foods were eaten at home or at a restaurant". Wow, wow, wow! You see how we are able to take on some many forms of indulgences unaware of its purpose, origination and effect. Yes, you my love, have increased in size because with or without your knowledge portion controls have increased in size. You also read correctly, these portion controls have increased in size no matter the location being a home or restaurant.

At the end of the day, you, like me, will have to "adopt your own diet strategies. You don't have to be a nutrition expert to be smart about controlling calories, for example, when eating out, avoid the complimentary bread they put on the table", or only eat half in the name of baby steps. "If fries come with your order, ask for a vegetable instead". Vegetables instead of fries is also a good choice if you know the week ahead is limited for exercise or extracurricular activities like a hobby.

Want another portion control tip for weight release? "Find other ways to socialize rather than eating out, during mild days, meet your friends at a park". In undergrad, my friends and I would soak up some park time or a beautiful, serene, walking trail like it was nothing. Now that we have Released All In Love and Trust, we've learned that portion control is about "adopting a healthy eating pattern", these are not temporary fixes, but lifetime strategies.

Let's Get Physical-Physical

Yes, Olivia Newton-John revved us up in the 1980s donning her hottest athleisure attire when she prompted us to get physical. I'll get to that level of physical that Olivia Newton John is speaking of however there are several tips to getting physical that does not involve the crisscross or any other dance move her video featured. What do I mean? The example of "taking the time to savor the aromas and flavors of your meal, as well as thoughts and feelings that arise while you eat" is a form of physical movement that is not Zumba yet will reflect on your fine figure. "Mindful eating has been linked with healthier food choices in restaurants. It can also help improve your self-control and prevent you from overeating". Yes, yes, yes, let's move on to more physical, physical!

1. Stay hydrated, hunger pangs can sometimes be misinterpreted, your body may actually be trying to tell you that you're thirsty. Drink water throughout the day, starting with a nice tall glass when you first wake up in the morning. You are less likely to overeat or reach for unhealthy snacks if you are properly hydrated".

2. Honey, treat yourself once again, "regular treats are an important part of a healthy eating regimen. Not only are you learning to choose more nutritious options, but also you are learning moderation and portion control", which ultimately leads to long-term weight Release.

Before I move along to the physical exercises through movement like yoga and dancing your ass off, while reading an article, Portion Size vs. Serving Size, I was able to find a "guilty as charged" on the list. I extend this to you because I am Releasing the behavior of "watching movies at home or at the theatre". No, no, no, not that easy, here is where Haven came to play. "Don't eat while watching TV or a movie or when you're on the computer. It's harder to control how much you're eating if you don't pay attention to what you're putting in your mouth, and when. At the movies, share a box of popcorn, and avoid the free-refill tubs and skip the candy".

O.k. Releasers let's move on to getting physical -you know, moving our hand to our mouth! "You need to know how to be successful in any food situation, you aren't going to stop eating out with friends, family and loved ones – you just need a strategy". Here are a couple of strategies for you that I will implement as well, yummy! "Order your meal before everyone else. Other people can influence our decisions without us really noticing. In social situations, people tend to mimic each other subconsciously, and dining out is no exception. People's menu choices and eating behaviors can be highly influenced by the choices of other people at the table. If you're eating with a group that is likely to order something that doesn't fit into your healthy eating plan, make sure you order first".

Please remember, when you are eating out, there are loads of hidden fat and sodium ready to take down the meal you so carefully selected. In the name of self-love, when you go out to eat with friends, family, co-workers, or wherever you may find yourself, you have to "customize, customize, customize! Don't be shy to ask for something prepared differently". Recall how I spoke on being able to say no, here's a chance to put that into practice with your weight release, "request that a kitchen holds a side dish and leave the sauces on the side. The goal of any venue is customer satisfaction".

As I move into how we break a sweat, physical, physical, I need to open up with a topic that I denied and ran away from for so long. As a matter of fact, the topic was touched upon previously in the book -rejecting the notion that when you look good, you feel good, my dear Releasers, that is the truth, so no more excuses for me.

What helped Release the truth, to the light I was rejecting, was a blog post titled "*I Traded My Old Shorts and Ts for Cute Workout Clothes and It Made Such a Difference*". No longer wanting to hide underneath a false thought pattern and belief, I knew I had to accept that the author of the blog was not coming for Haven. She was just willing to Release and be transparent, she states "this whole looking good while working out is something that's totally new to me, but I'm beginning to understand it".

Honey, she did not know how she made me free. I am able to begin the forgiveness work within myself for walking around looking so damn bad. It is very interesting to note that she put "no wonder I always feel so self-conscience in those classes – even if I love the workout. So I decided to try wearing something pretty". O.K. Releasers, I am up first and will start with enhancing my workout clothes, please keep me in your prayers.

When it comes to "engaging in exercise, whether your go to is sprints or dancing, or yoga, go sweat it out, this quells toxic emotions that can linger in our system". We have to know, there is an activity out there that's calling our name. Consider an activity you would love to engage in that's tailored for your personality, for example, I love to walk, it's the major method I used to release my weight. It's also an activity and taste that I acquired from my mother and her mates. Here's why, "walking modestly reduces body fat, it isn't going to get you shredded, ripped, cut, or yoked, but frequent walking will help anyone with two functioning legs and hip and knee joints".

Alright, so you need an incentive to walk, what about a natural, fine, round, behind? Yes, your glutes, you want a phatty like Beyonce and an ass like J. Lo's? "To make sure the way you walk is actually activating your glutes, place your hands on each glute. You should feel your glute tense up a bit with each footfall as it accepts the load, and that same glute should tense up even more when you push off to take another step so that your hand gets a little pushback".

Don't be concerned about getting this right your first couple of attempts, practice, practice, practice, as with our mental strategies, we have to do it with our physical strategies, you will get this! BlackWomenLosingWeight.com also offers excellent routines with a workout calendar and challenge to match so we can get physical, physical and enjoy a dope routine. One routine that caught my attention consisted of "jumping jacks, squats, kneeling pushups, and Russian twist".

Is there a low-impact, yet intense enough routine that you enjoy? What about a routine that may appear to be overwhelming, like weightlifting, yet you find the experience to be enjoyable? Released!

You're in your element, please, please, please, share, I am always looking for routines and I know our fellow Releasers would want in on the knowledge as well, look forward to learning from you!

Now that we have finished eating our piece of cake with a peace of cake, let's get excited and look forward to implementing portion control not in just what we eat but in our personal and professional lives as well. This mental strategy and course-of-action will allow you to observe and feel how much portion control and our lives connect.

A Peace of Cake & A Piece of Cake Release Reminders

» You can truly have and eat what you want, make portion control a constant companion

» While there is a whole pizza, we only consume a part of a whole, a portion, with control

» "Find other ways to socialize rather than eating out, during mild days, meet your friends at a park"

» Consider an activity you would love to engage in that's tailored for your personality, for example, I love to walk, it's the major method I used to release my weight

Bigger Fish To Fry

Now that I look back, my occupations have run the gamut and allowed me to have some incredible experiences, might I add adventures. One of my career moves was being a bank teller. It was during my days as a teller I learned the expression "bigger fish to fry". Yes, I was a bank teller, for close to 3 years, however trust, I was not Releasing All In Love and Trust, so I was still crazy, but back to the story at hand.

As you may or may not know, when you are employed at a bank, there are certain procedures and precautions that take place in case of a robbery or any type of emergency. One day during my check cashing days, my co-workers and I were sitting behind the teller line, and the opposite happens, the police pull up with their lights flashing, and a suspect, so we thought, was already in the backseat of his patrol car. Here's where it gets tricky, we had not been robbed, the gentleman, a known customer, had not entered the bank that day. So, why in the world would lights be flashing, and police be riding to the bank with a passenger, and not away from the bank?

Here goes, the young man was purchasing gas and ran short a few pieces of change, the police were phoned, and the young man explained to the officer if he took him right up the street to the bank, the matter could be resolved. Startled by his entrance, the young man filled us in on his very present circumstances and then announced, "I have bigger fish to fry, so I told the police officer to bring me here!"

It was then that I yearned for the meaning bigger fish to fry, why would someone, no matter fish to fry, ropes to jump, gas to purchase, want to be placed in the backseat of a lit up, patrol car. Idioms4you. com provided the best laugh out loud definition of the term, bigger fish to fry, "having bigger fish to fry means that you had better turn your attention to something that is more important". "Had better" put me in stiches!

My memory was lured back to the saying to tie in weight release. You "had better" turn your attention to cooking at home. Man, oh man, the benefits are endless, after a certain period in my weight release, my body begin to reject fast and low-vibrating food. It was then that I begin to fall in love with cooking at home. Here's the part where I have to pause and let you know that I do have to get much better with cooking at home because there are amazing benefits. "When you cook at home, you're in control of the food you cook and the food you consume. Preparing meals at home gives you the ability to exercise portion control and help curb the temptation of overeating".

Oh yes, we all need to eat at home, here's another reason, it "encourages family bonding". This is a great teaching tool for parents to instill healthy eating habits in their children. In fact, several studies conducted by the University of Michigan found eating family meals at the dinner table is associated with fewer psychological issues and higher academic success in children and promoted sociability in the family". Releaser's, with the days of social media and how we feel our values are being lost, this is an excellent benefit for eating at home -bonding with family and getting to know each other.

Want another reason why we need to fry bigger fish at home? It saves money, "eating dinner out is expensive! It is a lot more cost-effective to purchase groceries than ordering take out every night. While there is much controversy as to whether an individual meal is cheaper made cooking in-home than eating out, with nutritional intake and serving size accounted for, you will save a lot more money by eating in!"Me, oh my, the benefits not only help your waistline, it goes ahead and slides into your bank account. Now we are able to vividly observe the benefits of cooking at home, not only are your pockets taking a hit, by eating out, you are missing out on family time as well as being unaware of the food that enters your body. Another personal and professional advantage to cooking at home, is that it boosts your confidence and stacks you up on loads of intimacy.

Intimacy

You're in your element, your hair sits flawlessly, the music is flowing to your groove, with lit candles, the aromas from your meal matches well with the ambiance. As you reach for your 5 star kitchen knife set, you retrieve a stainless steel, sharpened knife, which you learned worked best for chopping vegetables, you effortlessly toss your hair over your shoulder, or maybe in a sexy gesture remove your hair from in front of your eyes. A gentle ring from the timer on your stove, allows you to grab your favorite kitchen mittens and open the oven to a scent even greater than your flow.

It's here that you have prepared a meal we all yearn for and the intimacy that we desire. Yes, cooking builds intimacy, not only will you connect with your family members, those of you who have a sweet thang, a honey bunny, or a crush, you can build and strengthen your relationship.

Here's why cooking and intimacy is a must, "in 1900, a paltry two percent of U.S. meals were eaten outside the home. In 2010, that number climbed to approximately 50 percent. Meanwhile, under 33 percent of families sit down for a meal with each other more than twice a week, on average, Americans eat 46% of their meals alone, when we do eat with other people at home, we often sit in front of the television or have to rush to the next task on the calendar". Yes, no space for intimacy, this is a problem for us, this is a space that our souls call out for on a familial, platonic, and Eros level. "Research finds that people who eat home-cooked meals on a regular basis tend to be happier and healthier and consume less sugar and processed foods, which can result in higher energy levels and better mental health. Eating home-cooked meals five or more days a week is even associated with a longer life". I want to pause and highlight mental health benefits, Releasers, if we are not healthy mentally or physically, there is nothing that can move forward in our lives, we have placed blockages on all sides. "Mental health benefits increase considerably when we eat home-cooked meals with other people. In fact, communal meals can make us feel happier even outside of meal times", that's a beautiful benefit. This is "partly because social connections reinforced over meals can help us cultivate a sense of belonging and even reduce symptoms of depression. Sharing the joy of home cooking also preserves cultural knowledge and history as we pass recipes from generation to generation". This is excellent, not only do you develop intimacy on a platonic and heart level, there are benefits on a communal level.

During our times together as friends and family you begin to develop your confidence and pride of self through recipes, fables, and life-lessons handed down from the ancestors. Here's another facet of home cooking I fall in love with and arouses the intimacy within me. "Buying ingredients from local farmers or grow your own". Everyone that loves me, knows about me, gardens, and agriculture, so its twofold for me. "You'll make an even bigger impact on the environment by significantly reducing the amount of transportation required to get food to your plate". Yes, bigger fish to fry by cooking at home is a plus! "Given that supermarkets offer a larger variety of foods than they ever have and the number of farmers' markets in the U.S. is at an all-time high, there's no better time to develop the habit of cooking meals at home". Also think of the benefit to your local community, those mom and pop shops that fall under small businesses.

Trust me, "keep it simple, don't feel as if you need to be a gourmet chef every night of the week. Start small and commit to cooking 1 or 2 quick, simple meals at home each week". Remember our success strategy to keeping it simple, would be to plan ahead for the week.

*Here's a juicy addition to all those benefits, cooking at home send signals and waves out to the Universe that you are ready for a family, if you are like me, marriage and motherhood are on the horizon. What better way to let the universe know that you are ready by starting in advance cooking wholesome meals for your husband and family.

Walking On Eggshells

Weight Release is not all about food, there are so many external factors that will cause your physical frame to react. This serving of our lesson shows how to apply walking on eggshells to weight release. Urban Dictionary has a definition that I find applicable to my expression "walk on eggshells" that is "to be in a delicate situation".

Autopilot has been released so when I use the term walking on eggshells, I'm not referring to a gentle, balancing act, however we once thought we were top experts and world-renowned researchers. Since we are Releasing, we need to proceed with our life and the lives of others, as if we are in a "delicate situation". There are non-verbal que's and actions we take that lead to weight release or its opposite weight gain.

I'll start with myself first to be in a delicate situation. Picture the scene with me in your mind, you may know the experience, you go to a beautician for the first time that's highly recommended by your friends. Internally, you experience serious trepidation, however you want to give it a chance, you want to finally find a home for your hair. Sure enough, you go through the wash and press or flat iron process, to realize that your greatest fears have been accomplished once again. Your hair is frayed and damaged, in addition to the letdown of something you hoped for, here is where we use to walk on eggshells the wrong way. Knowing that we hate our hair, knowing that we hated he or she's process, knowing that we hated how much they talked on the phone and to their fellow beauticians and staff alike. However, when asked, "do you like your hair? oh,

144

we all have been there and replied "yes" knowing that this was the first and last time you would ever visit that shop or salon.

The delicate situation that I speak of or walking on eggshells, is when it comes to eating, remembering to eat on a conscious level, autopilot no more. Remember those nonverbal que's and actions that I spoke of? During my days in the classroom, I had a terrible habit of skipping over breakfast. Man oh, man, did it have serious side effects! Running on fumes, I took my venting out on the kids and myself mentally because I was running low on food.

Here's the thing, you have to eat breakfast, "it (breakfast) provides your body with the fuel it needs to make energy to keep you focused and active throughout the day. If you are trying to lose weight, fueling your body regularly will help you from possibly making unhealthy decisions later in the day based on hunger".

Yes, by actually eating a wholesome breakfast, you Release weight, plus, your attitude and your occupation will say thank you. Here's another succulent to sit on the table or on the mantel in your mind. Guess what I told myself that I could not live without, if I did not have breakfast? Coffee, coffee, coffee! I know, I want to hear all your preferences with coffee! Mines, large, 11 creams, 9 sugars, I'll love you for it! However drinking coffee in the amount, I did –no portion control, yes even with liquids- added to my behavior, lack of energy, and lack of productivity, but most of all weight gain.

"Too much caffeine can interfere with sleep, make you jittery and cause you to lose energy later in the day", my loves, we have to let go, we have to Release. *5 Tips to Kick Bad Eating Habits to the*

Curb did not leave us stranded in the world of coffee. It states, "limit regular coffee to 3 cups or less per day, and watch what you put into it." Also if you want to wean off coffee, there are 3 suggestions – *"switch to half decaf or tea, drink plenty of water, and eat small, frequent meals to keep up energy".*

Who knew, all the yelling, all the frustrations, and the fumes I was running on, could have been solved by simply eating breakfast. Now I want to uplift a wholesome breakfast because for Haven, that was not always the breakfast case. An example of a wholesome breakfast would be a "whole-wheat English muffin with peanut butter", and my favorite because when I was little my grandparents would save them for me, is hard-boiled eggs, that's one of the main reasons I love munching on them to this day.

For me, especially in the genesis of my weight release, I loved frozen fruit, head over to your local grocer and see what types of frozen fruit they have available. This was an excellent step and method for me because I would wake up in the morning set the fruit out for the day and that allowed me to snack on fruit throughout the day instead of an unhealthy snack, please, please, please, give this a try. This step worked wonders for my initial 80 lbs. weight release.

I'm Proud of You

One way to successfully walk on eggshells, is to bring lunch, now trust, during my classroom days, you would not have been able to put a star next to my name for bringing my lunch. There were times when I actually prepared lunch or had leftovers, to only head straight out the door, and remember halfway to work that I left lunch in the refrigerator or even worse, on the counter, right by the door, on my way out.

Here is a solution, let's leave a neon sticky note on the door we walk through to leave for work. Here is where I got this strategy from, my mother's former occupation allowed her to tele-work several days out of the week, in order for her to remember her laptop when she headed into the office, she placed a neon, sticky note on the door she exited in the morning. Reminding her, "hey we are leaving, please remember this valuable asset, our tool for work".

Here is where Haven must make a confession, on the days that I did remember to bring my lunch to work, it worked out when I prepared the night before. Guess what? That whole day, I was shining through, you couldn't tell me a thing. Back to transparency, during my days of education, this was a goal I was not able to successfully complete and a costly habit. Yes, by not preparing your lunch for the week, you cost yourself tons of monetary value.

We are going to cease placing the hammer over our head, "how do you make bringing lunch to work easy? Have your arsenal of food for the week.By stocking up the fridge, you're setting yourself up for success". Wow, wow, wow! Here we go again with success, refrigerators and being properly prepared. Another tip that I have found successful and newsworthy whether you are in the classroom and regardless of occupation was "cook a batch of soup you can portion out for lunches or dinner during the week, or bake a whole chicken to slice for sandwiches and wraps". Now that sounds like a plan to me, I can't wait to tell you how it works out in my cookbook.

Before I let go, I want to assist you with your breakfast and other meals, Health.com states "breathe before you eat. We continuously breathe without thinking about it, but recent Spanish research showed that relaxed, controlled breathing can effectively reduce cortisol levels. Before each meal, take a few minutes to sit comfortably in a chair, and spend a few minutes focusing on breathing, slowly and deeply, in through your nose and out through your mouth." Talking about a mental strategy with a physical release.

Speaking from experience and in the name of weight release, with 2 previous jobs of mine, snacking was at a premium, that was a bank teller and an educator. During the holiday seasons, your customers and parents want to thank you through food and it's not always the healthiest. If you have a habit of snacking in general like me, then listen up, instead of "potato chips, let's go with pretzels and baked potato chips. Also, pickles, onions, lettuce, tomato, mustard and ketchup add flavor without the fat". For me, post weight release I also search for options that are healthy as well as filling. Baked potatoes came to the rescue because they "can be a healthy option, but have it with low-fat sour cream instead of butter". Let me know some of your snacking alternatives.

If You Must Snack, Here You Go

- Fresh Strawberries

- Regular or frozen grapes

- Pop-top cans of tuna

- Pineapple chunks

- Hard-boiled eggs

- Watermelon Cubes

- Apple slices

- Orange slices

Since I want you to be mindful and successful in all settings, I have provided some tips for a few of the settings where you enjoy dining. I will also include some affirmations that will go well with what you're eating. These affirmations are not to scare you off or sour your taste buds but for you to remain mindful, mindfulness helps us remain in a state of worthiness, peace, self-love, and in the now.

To walk on eggshells while you are dining out EatRight.org states "think ahead, consider meal options at different restaurants and look for places with a wide range of menu items. Check online menus, if available, for nutrition information ahead of time". Here is an easy baby step the National Heart, Lung, and Blood Institute claim's, "if you really want to have a soft drink order a small or sugar-free one". For dessert, no, you do not have to skip out, "order the smallest size of fat-free frozen yogurt, low-fat ice cream, or sherbet instead of cakes, cookies, pies, or other desserts".

Remember we are taking baby steps here, so as I always offer, you can do this every other visit, or back to the strategy of not eating the entire portion. Maybe this is the time you need to divide that dessert completely in half and save it for later, there's nothing wrong with leftovers. So what if your friends and family laugh at you, your waistline, your arms, your thighs, and your tummy will definitely scream thank you later!

Please do not worry or fret with these tips and suggestions, from experience, when you are Releasing All In Love And Trust, your mental and physical palate do the same and your taste adjust, your desire and hunger for more will expand in its proper direction. I don't want to turn you off from eating, here's why, I have discovered the beauty of food, it can be a method of healing as well as variety. "Salads make great meals, be careful of the dressing". Yes, yes, yes, we all love "fried chicken sandwiches however a blackened chicken sandwich" is best. I have mentioned baked potato's however let's reach for "potatoes without gravy, rice without gravy, cooked greens made without salt pork or lard".

As beautiful women, we love to let our hair down. Most of us have 40+ hour workweeks, motherhood may enrapture you or perhaps you are caring for your parents. At the end of the day, you are going to want to take a moment and get your Essence Fest on through Happy Hour time. Here are a couple of tips to help you wind down from your day in a walking on eggshells manner. "Try double appetizers. If there is a nice selection of seafood – and vegetable-based appetizers, consider skipping the entrée and having two appetizers for your meal. Often that is more than enough food to fill you up."

Here's another experience that has rang true with me. "Order a salad before ordering anything else on the menu". This worked wonders with my weight release, I once turned away from salad, now I turn towards it, salad aids with portion control and your overall meal.

"Scientists at Pennsylvania State University found that volunteers who ate a big veggie salad before the main course ate fewer calories overall than those who didn't have a first-course salad". My loves, dive into that salad, please remember to be careful with your toppings. You can actually do the reverse of weight release and that is not what we are here for.

Walking On Eggshells Release Reminder

» Walk on eggshells, remember we treat ourselves and others as if we are in a delicate situation

» Eat breakfast, it's your fuel for the day

» "Before each meal, take a few minutes to sit comfortably in a chair, and spend a few minutes focusing on breathing, slowly and deeply, in through your nose and out through your mouth"

» Healthy Snacks To Enjoy (they also can be purchased pre-sliced)

• Apple slices

• Orange slices

• Watermelon Cubes

Affirmations for Food

» All that is healthy and whole resides within me

» For the now, I am grateful

» I am a temple, to which I store health, food that enters this temple, follows the same

Thank you Jesus, for allowing to complete this passage. I did not know that you would call me however now I heed the call.

-This came to me prior to writing the passage and I decided to keep it in the book.

#IllAlwaysLoveMyMommaShesMyFavoriteGirl

Chapter 7
Get Those Steps In!

(Psst! Step To The Rhythm Of Your Own Beat!)

Get Those Steps In!
(Psst! Step to the Rhythm of Your Own Beat!)

Take some mental steps with me for a moment, this is a scenario we have all been familiar with. Be it the stairs in your home or apartment, walking up an incline at your job, running after your little nephew (wink), the moment you stop to take a breath, you notice that you need several breaths. Not only has the momentary action caused you to take several breaths, hell sometimes you need to pause or stop all together. One of my favorites use to be when I would be on the phone with a friend or family member, and they could tell by my breathing and tone of speech, there was some additional movement or requirement on my part. Laughing now as I would then, it would go like "you walking up a hill or something, you been chasing one of them kids?" Hilarious yet true, this was a common occurrence in my life. That being said, breathless occurrences due to obesity was something I wanted eliminated from my entire being.

Guess what the best solution was for me to Release those moments described above from my life? Yes, I had to, and have to, get those steps in! During my research for this book, I found that 10,000 steps a day was the current suggested number, here's the fabulous piece and peace for you and I. Be it 10,000 steps or not, always grab and take all steps possible. "To stay well, walk for 30 to 45 minutes nearly every day. Do it all at once or in chunks as short as five to 10 minutes." For instance, I lived in a second story apartment with parking spaces for the two buildings it housed. My nephews' mother offered me the dopiest advice "To get your daily steps in, park in the farthest parking spot". This advice was simple, money-free, and did not require additional travel but to my front door. Be clear, there were days that I loved and desired those extra steps from my car to front door. On the flip side, there were times when I had to remind myself of the rewards of this process and release any temporary thoughts and feelings of defeat or failure. Trust me, it's all to your advantage, before long, like me, this strategy will become second nature. Another layer of humor and motivation extended from this tip, is that for some time, my mother and cousin joined in on the fun. Often when my mother would come to visit me, she would park her car next to mine, to get her steps in as well.

The fun actually did not stop there with my steps, one of the multiple benefits of this practice poured into other areas of my life. When I am out running errands, now I don't need a parking space damn near at the front door or pound my steering wheel in frustration when there are no parking spots next to the handicap spaces. Yes, when we opt to get those steps in at all instances, you will be amazed at the petty variables that are released from your soul.

But Wait! Don't Do What I Did!
Hah! ;)

I am fortunate enough to have multiple sisters in my circle that have previously released weight. For example, when I first realized my weight Release journey was underway, my good friend recommended that I use a tracking device to monitor my progress. Let me tell you why this aspect is critical. For my initial weight release I did not add a supportive tool to track my journey, this step is imperative because it helps gain clarity with your body goals and to even tell myself or the next person the amount of weight I have released. As a case in point, your world is filled with people that you may not consistently run into, meaning those whom you haven't seen in a while (hey, we all have lives). A beautiful exchange and complete model strut follow, and then the big question comes "how much weight have you lost [I always remind that it's release]?" Instantly, you are a deer in headlights, "Who! What! A year ago, I stepped on a scale." Knowing your numbers helps you gain direction. Doing so, not only assists you, it allows you to be an asset to others.

Additionally, weight release tracking devices, are built-in confidence builders. Observing and charting your accomplishments shows YOU, how much YOU were and are able to achieve. Who's not going to stick their chest out, and smile with gleam when you can actually visualize all that you have earned? Another advantageous edge to this structure, is the opportunity to view your areas of growth, let's face it, there are certain areas of our body that soar with weight release. We also have those portions of our body that move a little slower, be it genetics or just a good old Achilles heel (these upper thighs and gut!).

Before I Let Go!
(In my Maze & Frankie Beverly voice)

Another incredible practice I employed is a beautiful habit I developed from my mother and her friends, walking the local park. Not only did I get to enjoy wonderful, juicy conversations with my best friend, my Mom (Mothers, I tell you!), nature obeys! What do I mean by nature obeys? My mind, heart, and soul get to absorb and observe the beauty of the park. Various and vast trees fill spaces, birds common to the area, send out their greetings and the human interaction is character developing as well as splendid. Yes, getting those steps in at the park with a loved one helps you Release weight in more ways than one.

For the Record

On average my mother and I walked the park about 3 days a week. Walking the park not only gets those steps in, its pure motivation. Think of the times, not just in the park, when you see someone giving their all to an exercise or sport. It not only instantly surges you with gratitude, it puts a pep in your step, causes you to tighten those abs and elbows, focus your stance, and gain concentration on your workout, even unto completion, hell, sometimes the motivation is so strong you do a little extra. What I am saying here once again is "get those steps in!" they motivate and inspire, increasing your gratitude and leading to more steps. When my mother and I first started walking the park, we only walked to a certain point. As we began to gain momentum with our steps, we started to say "you want to walk a little farther", even at times giving running a try. Now, we walk the full length of that portion of the park, not only in a much quicker time frame, but with grace, motivation, and enjoyment.

Word to the Wise:

Are you low on patience?
Does the slightest notion cause your emotions to elevate?
Do you fight like a participant on a reality t.v. reunion show?

157

Here's the solution for you!
"Walking"

"Walking releases natural painkilling endorphins to the body – one of the emotional benefits of exercise."

I Lied

Remember how I stated that getting your steps in led to more steps, well, I lied?! Those "more steps" actually lead to running. There have been several occasions where my mother and I have completed the walking trail in a shorter amount of time and just out of pure inspiration would jog to certain landmarks within the park. Let me interject, this is where you need the proper running socks and shoes. Please become informed about the art of running and at best, learn the basics. "When your feet are not able to function properly, other parts of your body must overcompensate, it is common to suffer from pain in the heels, ankles, knees, hips and lower back." My mother and I knew none of this while stretching our chops to running and our feet did NOT thank us later. In fact, know the type of shoe that works best for you. From aerobic shoes (walking is considered an aerobic exercise) to cross-training shoes, each shoe serves a varied purpose. "The American Orthopedic Foot and Ankle Society recommends that the type of shoe you choose should depend on the sport (or activity) you are most active in. If you perform a certain type of exercise 3 times a week or more, choose a corresponding sport shoe." Yet another reason to become informed, because sore, hurt feet, will not lead to you getting your steps in.

Let's Get It On
(In My Marvin Gaye Voice)

This is the action plan my friends, view your schedule for the week, next, research parks and locations most convenient to your areas of travel. Based on this knowledge, make a slight 10 to 15-minute adjustment to your day. Never schedule walking in the park (or any event for that matter) on days where it just will not work. One week you may be able to walk only twice a week, the next week your schedule will allow for 4 times a week, as stated in a previous chapter, schedule for your personality and life. Tidbit: Let's not limit are steps to just the park, incorporate activities you already enjoy, and ask a friend, sister, or co-worker to join you!

Walk, Yet Set a Realistic Exercise Routine

Not throwing caution to the wind, nor remaining rigid, a personal tip that I use, is to either set a timer or establish a distance I will reach within the park. The path and key to weight release is hitting your own personal goal. To illustrate, let us say you work full time, are a parent or in school, better yet all three. There will be days and periods of time where you flat out cannot get an extensive 60-minute workout in, here's the anchor removed, you do not need it! When you set your timer and walk 20 or 30 minutes or determine that you will walk to the second pond in the park for that day, you have just knocked out and completed a personal goal and task of the day. Who is prouder than you but you? You are elated, drifting back to memories and moments when you were the "man or the woman". Your chest sticks out like an action hero and "September" by the elements known as Earth, Wind, and Fire play in your head. "Right hand high for you" in my Lil Kim voice, daily goal achieved!

Bonus Features

Yes, like your fave DVD's, books, and downloads, there are bonus features to getting your steps in. To start, after accomplishing such a task-as getting those steps in and hitting your daily goal-you will not put just anything in your body nor your mind that jeopardizes your hard-earned results. Oh no! From experience, you will guard all that encompasses your universe.

Second, mental clarity will be more than a rare occasion, it will be a welcomed common occurrence. The daily on-going grog that followed me like a gray, rainy cloud above my head, I never missed! To the physical, a leaner body, with clothes that fit like a hand in a glove. Yes clothes! Especially with your clothes! We all have those designers that we adore, who only create clothes where the largest is a size 2. My loves, I am here to tell you, getting those steps in, now allows you to slide into those delightfully designed threads. Nothing has felt better than being able to walk into ANY store and purchase garments that I desire.

It's A Charge, Forward March!

Here's your charge to getting those steps in! Remember take time (preferably on a Sunday) to determine your schedule for the week. Doing so helps to determine how many times a week you will be able to work out, the work out spots most beneficial to your areas of business, as well as gears your mind up for the week. Don't forget to take note of the days you will be able to exercise and make the proper adjustments with your time.

Before I conclude, please take note of the days that you will not be able to work out (remember that is o.k.) and treat yourself to light, healthy snacks that day. There's no point in beating yourself up later on or the next day for not eating well with no exercise. Let us view this strategy as one of prevention, a prevention with bonus features.

Get Those Steps In
Release Reminder

» Walk, but set a realistic exercise routine

» Never schedule walking in the park (or any event for that matter) on days where it just will not work. One week you may be able to walk only twice a week, the next week your schedule will allow for 4 times a week, schedule for your personality and life.

» Park in the farthest parking spot of your destination as a strategy to achieve your daily steps.

» Weight release tracking devices are built-in confidence builders. Observing and charting your accomplishments shows how much YOU were and can achieve

» Weight release tracking devices also view your areas of growth, let's face it, there are certain areas of our body that soar with weight release. We also have those portions of our body, which move a little slower.

Don't Just Squeeze It In

And your off…, its Sunday night and the whole week is ahead of you, you know the meetings, deadlines, pick-up, drop-off schedules and the mandatories of your life. Here is where you have to slow down, you are releasing weight, you still have a schedule, be wise, your sub-conscious reacts wildly when stress like rushing, or squeezing things in begin to happen. Guess which wild side effect stress causes? We retain weight instead of releasing those mental and physical pounds. You making it through this entire book and journey let's us both know that weight gain is not your goal here.

I don't want to squeeze in words myself, so I will not be long, especially since the goal of this section is how to "shape your time" and not attempt to squeeze time into your priorities. A paradigm shift is what I am requesting from you here. "Being productive is all about preparation". We no longer have to cry out why God, no, we take our power back and make simple changes through baby steps.

Top 5 Don't Squeeze's Please
How To Plan

Now that we know we do not have to squeeze time into our priorities, I am going to leave you with my Top 5 Don't Squeeze's Please. Here's why there are only 5 steps, this is how to plan, we have to keep it simple. Once you Release and discover how those steps are connected and simple, you will soon begin to pump on all cylinders, making these steps a breeze.

Plan Your Outfits

For me this step could be oh so simple, yet it magnifies an ill trait that I am working on Releasing. I don't know about you but regardless of my size, I actually have clothes to put on. Here's the embarrassing fact, I forgot about my clothes because either I didn't wash, or they were not in their proper place to begin with. Be clear, these lack of actions, was to no ones fault but my own. Behavior modification is the order of the day.

When I look back on my classroom days, this was actually a very easy step. Teaching elementary school allows you to note, with the best intentions an 8 year old will be an 8 year old. To no fault of their own they will spill something on you, or step on your toes, things happen, so my outfits should have been a basic polo and khaki's, picture day excluded. Here's the thing for me, I couldn't wear polo's or a dress if nothing was clean or thrown all around my apartment. I need to be even more transparent because those were not just my classroom days, last week I lamented the presence of my clothes and apartment to myself, no, this was not in a good way. At the end of the day, in order for the week ahead to be successful, you have to plan for Monday on Sunday.

Create A Physical To-Do List

Here's the step that goes along with planning your outfits, create a physical to-do list, and no not write down your outfits and make them monochromatic. Take time to consider all your responsibilities for the week, this may seem weird especially if you are new to the practice, however your world will shift. When you create this physical list your subconscious matches that goal, you have established a hand to pen connection and your subconscious and the Universe are ready to respond. You will find yourself doing things automatically simply because you wrote them down and declared them a goal with the best intentions.

Be clear, it's allright if your first week you do not write everything down and follow your list in order, as with everything, it will take practice, you are a neophyte enjoy. "Your to-do list is, and will always be, fluid". Here's another beauty about creating a physical to-do list you are able to see what would be best for you to wear that day based on the things you have to do. We've all had those "I forgot" doctor's visits.

Here's What I Learned In The Process

Have you heard of input, output mode? Well I thank God for the penning of this book in more ways than one. During my research I discovered input, output mode and realized that's the system and flow all along. "Sundays should be input days –not output days. The start of every week is always output focused. It is advantageous of you to spend as much of Sunday as possible in input mode." This information right here caused some feelings of shame to rise, however I immediately released the thought and feeling because that is no longer me. "Having a great week does not start on Monday. It starts Sunday. It begins with what you set in your mind you are going to do, before you actually set out to do it".

"Have A Slow Morning"

My friends and family would more than likely laugh and consider every one of my mornings slow, God bless them! However, on Sunday, totally take this practice to heart, here's why, you are able to gather your thoughts and check-in with how you truly feel. It allows you to replay events from the week and place them in their proper place. Having a slow morning also allows you to not start and end your day on a jittery note. There's no point in walking around all jumpy and antsy simply because you did not take the time to arise slowly and enjoy the morning. This step is a plus because your mind and body will thank you, you are moving in flow and accomplishing what needs to be done. When you are in flow, you are better prepared to send and receive information. Take this step to heart because the way you wake in the morning plays a part on your day. If I'm up and at 'em grumpy, I will believe that everyone falls under the like –Not So! Take it easy and slow, there's nothing wrong with that, this is how we release weight and learn of our true selves.

"Take Time To Think"

If you really want to show yourself, how much you really love yourself, then taking the time to think, is the first signal of love. Your opinion is beautiful. We can start out with the best idea and intentions, yet when we don't take the time to think things through we experience explosions within our worlds. "If you do not take time to prepare, you will find yourself flustered and uncertain because you now have to think through whatever it is you need to do".

Here's the major peace that we are missing, and I feel why resistance is in place. We are scared to think what we think. You are so scared to think and voice your feelings, you don't want to take the time to consider your opinion. Now is the time to investigate why you do this, as a child where you placed in situations where this was the order of the day? Consider your answer and thoughts. At the end of the day you are perfectly human if you get angry or something causes you to cry, you have a soul and that soul has been touched. Not all of our thoughts and feelings that we ignore are bad. Times of glee, abundance of joy, can be shut out as well, luring us back to feelings of unworthiness. Oh no, not anymore, we take time to think. Thinking exposes how we truly feel and allows us to make the best choices for the day and our lives.

Know Yourself

While this should have been first, I purposely put it last because I need this to serve as a reminder for yourself when you are completing the above 4 steps. This is where self-love must kick in because you have to confess to yourself and others what you truly love -which is who you are. Now that we are Releasing and know that we are worthy to receive all forms of love, we know, that it is alright, if your favorite color is purple and orange and country music captures your soul, I'm a Rascal Flatts fan myself. Yes, those are the depths that you have to explore in order to be successful with knowing yourself and weight Release. No need to fear, the end results are amazing, you fall in love with yourself, I know cause it's me!

Don't Squeeze It In Release Reminders

» The wild side effect of stress -we retain weight instead of releasing those mental and physical pounds

» Plan Your Outfits - My outfits should have been a basic polo and khaki's, picture day excluded

» Create A Physical To-Do List -"Your to-do list is, and will always be, fluid"

» "Have A Slow Morning" -Having a slow morning also allows you to not start and end your day on a jittery note

» Take Time To Think -Your opinion is beautiful

» Know Yourself - Self-love has to kick in because you have to confess to yourself first and others what you truly love -which is who you are

Release According to Personality

As healing and Releasing begins, you will soon realize that you are a human being and have human being tendencies. Yes, you will find out that you once believed that you were not human. I know it sounds crazy, however, through your actions, these are the shock waves that were sent out to the Universe. Now that we recognize we are human, we crave structure and routine. Despite all the efforts society employs to have you believe the opposite, structure and routine bring you happiness and harmony.

Check-in with your personality to find out, who it is that you truly are. This allows you to create the proper groundwork for your structure. There's nothing wrong with your character or mine, we just have to create a routine based on our character. Want to know, how I know? Warren Buffett, yes, "the single most successful investor of the 20th century, that's worth over $70 billion", tells us to "schedule for your personality. Buffet doesn't like meetings, but he is building his businesses around his personality, doing it the way he prefers and enjoys. You will be most productive once you find what works best for you".

Scheduling for your personality, may seem so far fetch from weight release but trust me it works. Here's why, your personality can prevent you from releasing weight. Explore your personality so the proper blockages are revealed and released. I've found several blockages that can play a role in our weight release. "A growing body of research is finding intriguing connections between personality traits and habits that can lead to obesity. The same parts of the brain that control emotions and stress response also govern appetite. Early life experiences also set the stage for overeating years later, researchers have found".

The first logjam I selected pertained to me because I use to jump at something delicious whether it was food or clothes, to serve as an example, it's when "you're impulsive" that you reach the impasse of not being able to release weight. "The ability to delay gratification also relates to weight loss, says Art Markman, PhD, professor of psychology at the University of Texas. Eliminating little temptations will help: stop stocking your pantry with junk food and avoid the break room at work when you know there will be leftover treats".

Up next, I am still guilty as charged, so I knew it needed to make the list, "if you are often hard on yourself" once again, I am releasing with you. "People who lack self-compassion have a huge negative reaction every time they make a mistake. Those high in self-compassion simply move on and vow to not make the same mistake again."

While I am providing ways, your personality can prevent you from releasing weight, it is important to note, that I was able to locate an editorial that provides us with the contrast. Wouldn't you know it, I found myself on this list as well. Here's what I love about the Releasing experience, you discover that you are human, and there are ways out of your circumstances, no matter how daunting they appear. There are even personality traits that can aid in your weight release achievement. "Are you the one always keeping everyone in stitches? This attitude will become essential, at times when you'll need to roll with the punches. It will help you laugh at mistakes, small regains, mean-spirited comments, and bad days".

Mentor or Life Coach-My Personality

While we may have found ourselves on both list for our weight release success and failures, here's the antidote and as a matter fact I am an antidote myself, let's consider a life coach, like myself, or a mentor. This step will allow you to gain an "unbiased experienced opinion. According to a new personality study published by the American Psychological Association, people with personality traits of high neuroticism, low conscientiousness and impulsivity are more likely to go through cycles of gaining and losing weight throughout their lives as compared with others without those traits". Here is why a mentor or coach is needed "those who practice self-awareness have more self-control, make better food choices, and are less likely to eat when feeling stressed". In addition to gaining direction, a mentor and life coach will assist you in "clarity and goal setting. Life is very philosophical and you need to be pulled about occasionally to find out if your goals are actually aligned with what you want from life." These questions and more are what you will gain by seeking additional support for your feat.

Release According to Personality Release Reminders

» Check-in with your personality to find out, who it is that you truly are

» "Schedule for your personality"

» Your personality can prevent you from releasing weight. Explore your personality so the proper blockages are revealed and released

» Consider a life coach, or mentor to assist in your weight release and life goals

Chapter 8
Couch Potato To Hot Potato

Couch Potato To Hot Potato
Where Did That Come From

Consider the allure of a hot body and its tantalizing features, beautiful hair, long eyelashes, washboard ab's, a walk full of swag, yes, we all desire that picture-perfect body that we view from any form of social media. Then the record scratches and truth kicks in, you have developed into a couch potato and not the "healthy" Wendy's baked potato. No, this has morphed into a round belly, arms that wave hello with your hands, saddle bag thighs, and a raging attitude should an episode of your favorite series get erased from the DVR, yes, a couch potato. Here's the good news, its not just you and I, "a recent study found that more than 79.5% of men and 87.3% of women were sedentary", yikes and Ka-pow! Ladies let's not just glance over that 87.3% either, not only is it higher than men, with the roles and responsibilities we carry as women we must take care of ourselves first. You know the saying "happy wife, happy life" well if you yourself are not healthy enough to be happy and you are the wife, well, you are able to see the rest of the saying, you can take your power back. Here's why "if you're sedentary, you're doing to much sitting around and not enough exercising, and that combination may be putting you at risk".

It's also best to release this lifestyle because its origins will somewhat take you aback, at least it did with myself. "Tom Iacino of Pasadena, CA coined the term in the mid-1970s. Tom was a proud member of an organization combating the evils of healthy eating and exercise. What was the best way to convey his commitment to a sedentary lifestyle? Plant his posterior in front of the TV, of course, and chow down on as much junk food as possible"-NO THANK YOU. I would like to take a moment to highlight the benefits of researching and finding information out for yourself. Think of the countless habits and sayings we have acquired only to find out that, with it's origins, we disagree. Yes, you have to find out for yourself, while I thought that I was smart prior to penning my book, the research required to speak on this subject opened my eyes to worlds of new and exciting information.

Couch Potato No More
It's Not What You Think

Here's what's ever the more about Releasing couch potato lifestyle, it's not what you think. Shortly after it clicked mentally for me that my weight release had taken place, I was able to finally view my shape and figure for what it was- a couch potato no more. Here's what prompted this section, one day while enjoying an afternoon with my mother, a commercial promoting only the hottest (of course) of elliptical training, displayed a stealth, muscular, young man giving the machine his best, I mean, sweating and in rhythm to the machines highest caliber yes, he was getting it as if his life depended on that training session. While we were viewing the intense workout, it was then that my mother said to me, "I know you glad you didn't have to do that to lose your weight!" I glanced up and down my frame and quickly agreed, don't worry, I also let her know that I didn't lose my weight I Released it and you will Release your weight (mental and physical) as well!

That's why we are here, in order to level up from couch potato we do have to put some moves in, however, it does not have to be to the intensity of a professional athlete or your friend who hits up the gym 5-6 times a week since undergrad. No, we are not talking that at all, you are able to view my before and after pictures and that was not the case. Instead, invite low impact exercises into your life. For example, with my weight release, I walked the park with a steady pace alongside my mother. There was a sidewalk that ran about a mile long close to my home, and at least 3 days a week you would be able to find me there. The list is endless of low impact exercises and activities, it just does not have to be gym related. "Determine when you watch TV: is it early morning, the middle of the day, after dinner, or late at night? Map out these times and begin searching for better activities that could replace TV during those times".

Healing & Leveling Up
Be Calm, Surgery is Taking Place

Here's the thing Releasers, when you make the decision to change-couch potato to hot potato, a shift has to take place mentally, we were not taught that some shifts will take massive mental moves, what I mean is, if you are not attached to a medical machine or bleeding from a gunshot wound we have trouble comprehending what is going on with ourselves and others. Be calm, surgery is taking place! Yes, I know that we are used to the physicians, anesthesiologists, nurses assistants and the staff needed to perform any type of surgery, however, this is what's going on with you mentally to Release couch potato, so you have to be easy with yourself. In 5 Tips to Help You Break Your Couch-Potato Habits, you are encouraged to take a bath. "According to Health.com, taking a bath connects you to the time you were the least stressed (in the womb) and reduces stress. Pick a bath bomb or scented Epsom salt to soak with; these have stress-reducing properties that are also great for your skin". With autopilot now being released from my mental this tip rings true. Consider the times you took for yourself and soaked in the beauty of a luxurious bath, taking the time to caress every portion of your skin and even basking in the afterglow that a bath invites, yes, take a bath, and I will take one as well, let's light some candles to enhance the ambience.

Visualize Where You Want To Be
Nothing Is To Good To Be True

As with all things in life, weight release included, you must visualize where you want to be. For example, some of you reading this text may simply want to Release 20 pounds and restore your pre-baby figure, some may be in my Releasing spot to the tune of 80 pounds, whatever your goal, you have to visualize the desired results. Perhaps you do not want to put a number to your weight release and create a goal of being able to seamlessly slide into your garments. How about my personal visualization of being able to walk into any retail store and purchase items from any section of my choosing. Let me tell you how wonderful and dream-come-true this felt, when this visualization came to fruition, my emotions were overflowing, trust me, if you don't get a hold of yourself during this experience, you will find yourself "crying like Tammy Faye Baker". My next visualization level-up is to be able to purchase whatever I want from a department store, there is no cap to my spending. I want to know about your visualization, what prompted you to select this goal and create this visualization.

Trophy Is Decoration
Not Size

I have fallen prey, so this must be stated, being a trophy is decoration not size! Rightly so we have fallen prey to the ills that society places on women, oh, all the things you have to be and all at once, absolutely no room for error. Right? No, here's the part we leave out - we our human so an unrealistic rulebook will not work. You have to know that you are whole, complete, choose able, lovable, of supreme status that is a trophy-you. Where we run into confusion is when we are told what exactly a trophy is and has to be. Naturally you are going to start observing what is titled a trophy and take note of the differences with you.

Growing up, my dad hung around a lot of ball players, their heights would easily range from 6'5 to 7 feet, however, at best, their girlfriends were 5'4, hell, I was probably dam near 6 feet by the 8th grade, with that being said and in my mind, yes, I told myself this, tall men only like short women. What in the world was I going to do, by the time I met most of my "play aunties", I was towering over them or soon to be, this thought totally fucked me up (so I thought) because I was doomed forever, a tall man would never look my way-true story.

Here's where it gets better, not only where these women short, they were absolutely beautiful and ran the gamut, different complexions, styles of dress, and accents from all over the world, talking about a ugly duckling compared to a swan. This is the thing, nothing is to good to be true, I will state that again, nothing is to good to be true, that trophy wife or trophy young lady you yearn to reflect, it's yours. It does not matter your size or all the obstacles that appear to be in the way. Being a trophy is about decoration and how well you are able to reflect your personality through your style of dress and the way you carry yourself. When I look at old pictures of myself I cringe and have to Release my inner guillotine. Now I see why my friends where like what the hell are you talking about there's nothing wrong with you, I was a trophy, I had yet to learn that trophy is decoration not size. "Thoughts are not facts. The negative voice is the part of you that has internalized all the warped messages thrown at you by society since birth and works overtime to shame you into fitting in with societal norms".

Her #Trophy

Trophy Challenge

Since nothing is to good to be true we are going to put ourselves to the trophy challenge, "instead of buying into what you internalized over decades in this place, I invite you to challenge what you've learned. What is learned can be unlearned–with practice". I want to see some pictures of you getting your trophy on! Please log online and share.

Act "As If" You Already Are

Just as sure as I look back at my old pictures and now see the beauty that those around me where able to see. The same applies to you – believe you me, when you begin to Release the mental back up, all the stale, old, lies and notions you believed, your vision for your physical, will follow your mental. No, your hot potato body has not arrived yet, however you have to prepare and act "As If". Here's the thing, you must act "As If" because you already are! Where were you when the 90's cult-classic Clueless hit the silver screen? Alicia Silverstone, playing Cher Horowitz, has a scene in the film, that makes me belt out laughing to this day and I apply this to all areas of my life. Cher shoves a guy away from her in complete disgust and laments "As If" as he attempts to approach her in a romantic gesture. The poor, young, guy wasn't just shoved away in rejection, she had a twisted facial expression, shut-off body language, and a tone that matched her words, no, her "As If" was sure and confident – you have to do the same.

You have to know and believe – "As If" – to any form of worry, doubt, shame, fear, impatience, sadness, remorse, guilt, shame, you know your Release. To the same effect, the hot mind and body you deserve is real, so you have to act "As If", none of those other lower vibrating frequencies are real, Release your belief in them and they will disappear from your life.

Kimora Is My Idol
However…..

Since we are visualizing and acting "As If" there are few pieces of advice that I want to drop in your ear, this is pivotal because I was beating and battering my soul and body from this one misconception, when you select your visualization piece make sure this person is in somewhat correlation with your shape and goals. Here's why, Kimora is my idol however height aside I don't think even post weight release I could fit a blouse of hers and that's after she's had 4 babies. Laila Ali is around my height and has a fuller build so that's who I would check for, her style of jeans and what pieces of clothing she wears to promote her best features. Ashley Graham is another Hubba, Hubba, who I love to check for, and the ultimate goal for me is Anansa Sims, she gives me the reasons, Anansa can boldly rock a two-piece bathing suit with sheer confidence. I never even considered wearing a two-piece bathing suit until I saw her rock that garment like it was her own skin-in real life those 3 to me are like goals!

Act "As If" Release Reminder

» When you are exercising and eating, act "As If" you are Laila Ali

» When your confidence is waning, and false, negative, thoughts appear, act "As If" you are Anansa Sims in a two-piece swimsuit – "I Am the supreme being, All That Is, resides in me!"

» When you have to put in to practice style, class, and phuck what you heard, act "As If" you are Ashley Graham

» "Thoughts are not facts"

Reach for these beliefs and affirmations when trying situations arise

TRUST ME, THIS IS LIFE, YOU WILL HAVE TO USE YOUR "AS IF"!

Take a few days to consider some role models and mentors within the field of your heart's desire who you can emulate. *Please remember to consider items like height, body type, and your personal field of dreams.

Once you take the time to figure out who these pivotal characters are, jot them down in your Release workbook, chit-chat with me about it online. We may share a kindred spirit in a mentor or two!

Couch Potato to Fitness Enthusiast

This headline from a blog captured my attention because I love how they used the term enthusiast and not fanatic. We have to Release the belief that it has to be all blood, sweat, and tears with weight release and with life - no one is asking you to train for the Olympics. Instead let's become enthused. One definition for enthusiast states "a person who is highly interested in a particular activity or subject". With that said, I will leave you with these 3 tips to propel you into a fitness enthusiast.

Watch What Goes Into Your Mouth

This one, is for me, and regardless of size -it's everything. During my initial days of weight release, I came to the realization that I really didn't give a damn about what I put in my mouth (pause), this was really eye opening to discover since food was my main go-to to relieve stress and drama in my life. Fast food and super-bowl party favorites are saturated with all the wrong ingredients that will expand your waistline and turn on the couch potato signal. "Everything you're stuffing down your throat is meant to taste good; crisps, junk, confectionary, ice-cream, beer, and fizzies, any and everything possible to make you feel happy in your spot".

Be More Social Not Media

Please remember there is an actual world outside your phone, we are not putting everything on technology and Netflix. Releasing the bondage, you are in with your cell, allows you to discover far more beauties. Those majestic places you view on Google images are real. So real, that you can visit them, trust me, your Higher Power wants you there that's why He created them and you! While you may need to renew your passport (hand raised), I have some local suggestions to get you on your way, these are sure to spark some ideas within yourself.

- Paint & Sip – I watched a paint and sip on Instagram and they were rocking out to Knuck If You Buck by Crime Mob

- Film Festival – Don't sleep on indie films, my brother turned me on to this vast intriguing world – I want in!

- Art Exhibit – Creatives unite!

- "Walk a newly renovated area of your city with a group of friends or someone you want to get to know" – Some new edifice is always popping up in my town

Enjoyable Low Impact Exercises

- Rowing – here's the thing, I don't know for how many years I was looking at a row machine and did not know what it was, I was able to locate a 30-minute workout online that I can't wait to try!

- Step Aerobics – "for a good cardio workout without all the pounding, science suggest signing up for a step aerobics class. Researchers found an hour of step aerobics gives you the same workout as a mid-distance run".

- Swimming – this is an oldie but goodie to me because it put me in the mind favor of rounding up several of my girlfriends and enjoying some fun in the pool in addition to endless chatter about the color mauve and what is our best angles, you know, the essentials!

Gilded Not Glitter

"All of this would not be possible without sponsors like yourself!"

Where were you when your favorite tv show concluded its episode or you had the viewing pleasure of public access television when an announcement similar to the one above blared through your tv or radio? It took me forever to understand what exactly this meant. Here goes the best description I located. "A TV sponsorship is essentially an opportunity to showcase a brand in a frequent and, relatively, non-intrusive way".

Here's where you and I tie in, we are our own tv sponsorship, and couch potato to hot potato will not be possible without sponsors like yourself. What do I mean? Couch potato to hot potato will not happen with lower thoughts, take control of your thoughts, they have to be gilded not glitter. Glitter is "tiny pieces of plastic broken down to a minute particle", no one wants their mind, body, and soul to be tiny pieces of plastic, no we create and pursue glided thoughts, thoughts that are "made from or covered with gold".

"Teach others to respect you, not like you"

In order for your thoughts to become gilded, first "identify thought patterns that lead to unwanted feelings". Here's an example, that prior to my weight release, caused an early time of trouble in my life - "teach others to respect you, not like you". This was a serious line for me to draw, because, I Haven, believed in so much lack, i.e. not enough friends and juicy people who would love to share their space and time with me and vice versa. Now there is a continual, attitude of gratitude and commitment to Release the unwanted, unnecessary belief and behavior of lack. "We all want to be liked, but when being liked is top priority, we often compromise ourselves. We, women, are not schooled on setting boundaries, which leads to overcommitment, resentments, and all-out exhaustion." Here's the thing, teaching other to respect you, must start with you and I, it starts by creating and seeking those thoughts covered in or made from gold.

#YepthatsmyhairandIcombeditthatday

By the way, do you want to know why those ads and announcements run when they do? "Some of the most effective slots are the ones that happen at the top and tail of ad breaks. Running right before viewers leave the room, or as soon as they come back, these ads are likely to reach a wider, more engaged audience".

Gilded Challenge

When couch potato, not hot "gilded" potato thoughts creep into your mind, please remember if it's an unwanted feeling, it was led on by an unwanted, non-gilded, couch potato thought.

Couch Potato To Hot Potato Release Reminder

» In order to level up from couch potato to hot potato we do have to put some moves in, however, it does not have to be to the intensity of a professional athlete

185

» As with all things in life, weight release included, you must visualize where you want to be

» You have to prepare and act "As If" because you already are!

» Being a trophy is decoration not size!

» Take control of your thoughts, they must be gilded not glitter

Get A Hobby Why Don't Cha
It's Where The Healing Kicks In

I'll be the first to admit that when I hear the word hobby, visions of pocket protectors and old-head political comb-over's dance in my head. While I am reaching for humor to express my point, if you were ever like me a collection of rare bottle caps nor postage stamps from the antebellum era never tickled my fancy. However, to set the hobby record straight, on a proper enlightening tone, the Universe needs to use you as a vessel for the greater fulfillment of your life and others. When you complete your fulfillment by caring for yourself and others you allow your very own healing to kick in. What better way to receive your heart's desire than pruning a talent that strikes your interest?

In an effort to create an arousing section on hobbies, I looked up the definition. Merriam-Webster contained two, so I will be specific, because I don't want you to purchase a small old-world falcon, if you must, please make sure that it is dark blue above and white below with dark streaking on the breast, don't want you to be deceived, those sellers on Amazon can get tricky you know!

However, I do want you to receive the ever-present gift of healing so the second definition for hobby was "a pursuit outside one's regular occupation engaged in especially for relaxation". Take note of the word relaxation, look how much your Higher Power wants you to grow, evolve, and heal, He or She has provided you with a way out through peace and mental repose.

Hobby Me A Benefit

Now that we've learned hobbies can be a solution for healing, naturally we want to explore what are some actual benefits of finding and maintaining a hobby. Regenerative Medicine Solutions states "an abundance of unreleased stress can be incredibly detrimental to one's health. Worse yet is the fact that unplanned time can be wasted. Whether it's spending ten free hours to binge-watch a season of Game of Thrones or spending those same ten hours to learn how to swim, our time is a critical resource to all of us, so it's best to use it productively".

This hits home for me because I would be the first one to holla out that such and such said this or that because they are rich, when the truth is, at some point, one of the greats you encounter had to put in sweat equity aka use their time wisely before a dollar of their millions was earned. Even closer to home, regardless of my bank account, as a writer, I need to be writing on a daily basis, Releasers-I am still growing to write daily, that is a "time is a critical resource to us all, so it's best to use it productively" example.

Maybe writing is a hobby you select, perhaps tennis is bouncing around your mind. I have selected several areas of our lives where hobbies would be beneficial. Another purpose of this section is to spark your interest in the direction you would like to head when considering a hobby. Trust me, the benefits are endless when you commit your time and energy to a therapeutic engaging activity.

Getting My Hobby On through selfies, yes, I'm still learning how to do so

Spiritual

In my pursuit to heal and obtain the true meaning of life, I finally caved in to the world of self-help, this world, that was calling my name for years, finally had the chance to emerge when I resigned from my teaching position. Here's what I learned, my mind was chucked full of shit just as much as my waistline, I was religionized in addition to being Bitch 101 and 102 and needed a way out. It was then that I reached for the readings of Florence Scovel Shinn, my cousin recommended her readings years prior and I even went then and purchased the book off Amazon, yet it was years before I absorbed its content, I personally am able to crack her readings open now and walk away with a new light and meaning every time.

While absorbing the information available to me for Releasing All, I discovered a platform to increase my knowledge on the events that were taking place in my life and to help my readers. I became a certified Life Coach the journey was worth it and incredible. Not only am I able to add a layer of understanding through experience, life coach training allows me to guide the way in an informed tone- being able to guide and control your emotions and your emotions not leading you around. Here's where the Universe rises to meet you, during my Life Coaching studies I developed the confidence to begin certification courses in yoga and meditation. Was I scared and under the impression that those courses would be full of terminology that even the curators didn't know, heck yeah? Here's what was even greater, it was all an illusion and the courses were created by someone like you and me. Those wanting to Release All In Love And Trust, who sat their fears aside and went for it, be willing to explore your hobby through a certification, I promise you, its not what you think and well worth it, let me know!

Mo' Money Mo' Money Mo' Money

Who here wants a career boost? Well guess what, selecting a hobby will increase those chances. My mother and Sister Friend's know I am an online, short, course fanatic, anything to advance my knowledge in the direction I'm heading. Here's what happens when you turn those courses into a hobby, in **3 science-backed reasons having a hobby will help your career,** "having a creative hobby is associated with positive work-related traits, like creativity on projects and a better attitude on the job. Other research shows that employees with hobbies are more satisfied with their jobs and have a lower likelihood of burning out". What if one of those hobbies manifested into your new career? Mo' Money Mo' Money Mo' Money!

Networking

Let's move on to another area where hobbies will be a benefit to you both personally and professionally. Who here knows everybody in the world and you know everyone especially as it pertains to your area of interest? It's safe to say you probably don't know quite as many people as you need to know. Top that as well, with discovering you need to get out way more just to be a normal human being. I think the latest dance I know is the dab. I'm landing on both of those lists. Here is where a hobby kicks in, not only with networking, are you out amongst people, in my case networking is essential because I am an author and entrepreneur, I need to have my face out there to spread the word about my brand. What area or field are you in? More than likely networking will be one of your best marketing tools to advance your heart's desire.

Love Interest

While you are out there networking and enjoying your hobby let's not skip over the opportunity for you to meet someone. You never know what cutie will be at the next archery class. Also, since you are willing to be open and explore a hobby, be willing to step out of the box with your preferences to a love interest. We all know and have fallen for someone who was not our supposed types. This just isn't for my single cuties, this applies to married couples as well, think of how your marital bond will be strengthened when you build confidence together learning a hobby. For example, when I get married, I want to take dance classes with my husband to give his own feet a lifetime break from mine and to show him how willing I am to be vulnerable in front of him, cause trust me vulnerability will be at play when I begin my dance classes.

Weight Release

Here we go, the point of it all, weight release! I'm telling you, I was not aware of the benefits hobbies played on weight release, here's the other cool thing, these activities don't have to be rigorous activities and sports. The major point for hobbies is to remove your mind and body from stressful situations so the Universe can work out whatever is going on in your life, and it's all right with whatever is going on in your life. We do not what to go out of the frying pan and into the fire, this will defeat the purpose of a hobby. Here is where I'm going, if your mind is consistently focused on weight release especially in a negative tone, you are all in the way for the universe to release your weight. Those finite thoughts you consume, those limited beliefs, Releaser's the Higher Power you serve has your life under complete control. He/She needs none of your help, your consistent negative focus on weight release is clogging all the channels. What can make its way through a clogged system of any kind? There is a way out or unclogging and a hobby can be one of those ways. As with everything in life, weight release and hobbies included you are not going to start off like Usain Bolt in his prime, meaning, you may put in sincere effort for your weight release and hobby but initially experience meager returns, this is the process, do not give up. When we were first born, an infant, we were not expected nor required to have a complete dialog with our parents nor pop out of the womb walking free of any assistance, apply this same belief here, you are simply a neophyte, like all, and that is not a permanent stage, in fact, it's quite the opposite, it's just the genesis.

Here's Why, You're A Creative

Here's the deal, do you want to end up in the belly of a whale? Yes, I do believe the story of Jonah and the whale was real, here's why, who here has made a decision that had them feeling at minimum that they resided in the belly of a whale? I can wave both of my hands and stomp my feet. Here's one of the reasons why, you're a creative. You know, all those weird people, who are just different, most things don't move them like the masses, taste and interest are surely not like the rest, their preference is calm, yet a raging storm can happen at any moment, you know just plain old you and me.

While we can laugh, it's us and that's perfect, yes perfect, you see your Higher Power created you and I for a purpose and we can't be like the rest. Accepting that you are a Creative allows you to understand the Creator wasn't coming for you in a bad way, He created the mold for creatives, with you in mind. Creatives likes, tastes, and interests must be set in this manner i.e. you and me, so a legacy can be fulfilled. Yes those idiocrasies you practice, that extra sensitivity, the desire for abstract art, that's everything you need to be in order to manifest the Creative that you already are, trust me, one of the reasons Jonah ended up in the belly of that whale was because he rejected the Creative that was him. However, like Jonah, and in love, we can embrace who we are. This allows us to Release our low vibrating whale belly belief, who wants to pay rent or mortgage there?

Signs You're A Creative

Before I let go, I must let you know that there are powerful signs exploding in your life that you are a creative, please explore and further your research on this topic, you are doing yourself a disservice if you do not. Here's why, you can be walking around beating yourself up over a quality that you actually need to fulfill your life's purpose however if you don't take the time to receive the information available you will be walking around committing internal suicide for no reason. Here's the other thing if you are not taking the time to identify your emotions, know who you are, and examine what you truly like and love, you are moving in the opposite, opposite, opposite direction of your life's purpose and heart's desire. I put heart's desire because that man you want, myself included, might be in the opposite direction you are headed. What are YOUR daily activities that would attract that man to you, and I'm not talking just aesthetics here, what about your attitude, where are you with your career, what are and how are the state of your finances? Examine your home, is it clean (yikes for me), have you prioritized and went grocery shopping? Spiritually where are you, what level of depth do your conversations contain or do your conversations reflect no depth at all? These questions and more are what I had to answer, remove, and Release from my life before anyone came along, and as I am writing this book, not everything that I mentioned above is crossed off that list, for example, I can't wait to have a maid come through at least 2-3 times a week, I'm just being honest in my Future voice.

Here's the thing, our goal here on earth or during our lifetime is to achieve a soul's purpose, there is no point in fighting that Universal Order, however we can go with the flow of the tide and allow our personality and gifts make a way for us. Below I selected an article that describes some traits of a Creative, titled 41 Signs You Are A Creative Soul read on to determine if you see yourself in some of the traits listed below.

Signs You Are A Creative Soul

- "You see talent in others, even when they can't recognize it themselves

- Your dream career is in a creative field, even if you're not in that line of work,

- You are inspired by the natural world"

Apple Doesn't Fall to Far From The Tree
Creative Traits from My Mother

Here's the beautiful thing with healing and discovering who you are and who you were meant to be, your Higher Power allows you to see the traits you inherited from loved ones you must forgive. Let me be transparent here, I'm speaking of forgiving my parents, in this case, yours may look different. Here's why I feign for healing and forgiveness, the minute I began to clear up my unforgiveness for my mother and father the natural talents I inherited from them begin to arise and develop in a colossal way. Forgiveness and healing allowed me to observe how some of my talents arrived, like public speaking and interior decorating, that was bequeath to me from my parents.

You may also be a creative and inherited quality traits from your parents, however you rejected the notions and signs within your life, due to your relationship with your parents. No more, we, you and me, have finally put a stop to cutting off our nose to spite our face, especially over **someone else's actions**, we now cut the cord. Below, I provided some signs and actions we take in life, that lets you know, you are a creative. Please explore this list and see where you fall with your parents. As always continue your research and personal development journey, you will discover far more than I have and fall in love with yourself during the process.

"You're sarcastic.

Yeah sure, sarcasm is great for your career. Everyone just loves a sharp-tongued smart aleck. But wait, I'm not actually being sarcastic here. Studies show that sarcasm is a sign of intelligence as well as creativity and can be a good predictor of career success."

"You're easily distractible.

Being unable to focus sounds like a bad thing, but according to science being easily distractible is also a sign of creativity. Real-world creative achievement was associated with leaky sensory processing or a reduced ability to screen or inhibit stimuli from conscious awareness."

"A Hobby Can Be Anything You Put Your Mind To"

That's right Releasers, a hobby can be anything you put your mind to, so let's get started, I compiled a list of hobbies that grabbed my attention and in the future I will give them a try, some on the list I have already completed and made an attempt, for example I took belly dancing classes with my mother, however I mentioned a time or two that I am Releasing two left feet so that's what I mean when I say attempt, lol.

List of Hobbies

Writing Archery Scrapbooking Create Collages Cooking-Healthy Mindful Eating Running Jogging Join A Club Learn A Foreign Language Jewelry-Making Candle-Making Belly Dancing Painting Drawing Toastmasters Public Speaking Sewing Photography Gardening Kayaking Volunteering Surfing Pole Dancing Floral Arrangement Aromatherapy Creation Pottery Sculpting Doll Making Soap Making Podcasting Mixology Astronomy Acting Biking

Chapter 9
Don't Eat A Butterfnger Be One

Don't Eat A Butterfinger, Be One

As we round the bend on our Release, I want to equip you with my Butterfinger strategy to move you along the way. The notion of a Butterfinger was trigged from my childhood when I would spend summers in Cali with my father. During the week when he was at work, he would call shortly before quitting time and ask my brother and I what we wanted from the corner store or gas station, more times than not I would say a Butterfinger. It got to the point that if he didn't call, he would still show up with my Butterfinger. Let me pause to say that had my mother been around, she would not have been down with daily Butterfingers, especially in the name of a 10 year old. My mother would have shut that practice down to once a week or weekends should I exhibit the proper behavior; you know the evil things that mothers do.

Here's why we are here, when it comes to weight release, you have to be a Butterfinger, not eat one. Now you betcha I believe that you are as "crispitycrunchity" sweet as a Butterfinger, however I need you to switch over to the metaphoric sense of the term. Yes, that butterfinger, when you can't grasp, or get a handle of an item, person, place, or thing, "you are carrying or trying to catch".

For example, LeBron James is one of my favorite professional athletes, just think if LeBron consistently had butterfingers, do you think we would be hearing his name, what about his 3 NBA Championship rings? More than likely, having butterfingers in any type of sport, not just in basketball, will get you a grand opening and grand closing all in the same night.

With weight release we have to be butterfingers, we have to let food, slip through our fingers, especially when our body is signaling that we've had enough. Years ago at one of my attempts with weight loss and not weight release, a friend of mine taught me a valuable lesson in being a Butterfinger, not that I couldn't eat one.

On a roll with working out and caring for my figure, I would join in on some after work exercise. Within two weeks of working out at least 3 times a week, I was able to release 4 pounds. I was so excited, I felt I deserved a treat or two, or however many the box contained, let's just be honest. Here is why you need friends, excited about my weight loss, I grabbed a whole box of snacks, it was then that my friend told me, "don't get the whole box of snacks Haven, just buy one". Wow, wow, wow! Not only was he showing me how to have butterfingers, he showed me I can eat what I want-just lean on portion control.

"Bottom line, an overloaded plate can lead to an overloaded stomach. Big portion sizes can mean you're getting more food than your body can stomach to maintain a healthy weight. Learn how much to put on your plate to help control how much you eat." The same goes for the unhealthy snacks I spoke of, being a Butterfinger means portion control.

Here's A Butterfinger

The constant talk of Butterfingers made we want to learn some cool facts about a candy bar that rocks my world. No pun intended, the facts were delicious. "In order to get that rich flakiness, the recipe calls for the addition of corn flakes! Now, these aren't your

200

regular breakfast flakes. These are light, airy and the perfect oomf to give the smooth peanut butter a bit of body". Want to know what gives a Butterfinger it's orange tone? O.K., you twisted my arm, its molasses, how yummy!

Although I spoke of Butterfingers to bring our physical solution home, there are other ways that you can be a Butterfinger and not eat one. "Add veggie fillers. Bulking up your meals with veggies is one easy way to cut calories while filling you up fast. Spinach, for example, can be used as a sandwich-topper or can add fiber and nutrients to pasta and stir-fry".

This next strategy on how to be a Butterfinger with weight release was one of the biggest reasons, I remained overweight. In order to eat your meals in a proper manner, you have to "limit mealtime distractions". For example, are you an "office dweller? Consider taking your lunch break away from your desk –in an American Journal of Clinical Nutrition study, people who played computer solitaire while having lunch felt less full at the end, and went on to eat more food later in the day than those who didn't play the game".

Now that we are able to grasp the meaning of having butterfingers when it comes to food, I want to leave you with a tip from 10 Easy Portion Control Tricks because this has saved me and I actually enjoy the activity. "Measure accurately. For foods and beverages, use gadgets like a measuring cup, tablespoon, teaspoon, or food scale". How superb, this releases the guessing game of measuring your food accurately and even keeps us in line with our seasonings. With that said, "proclaim your freedom. Now that you're getting back on track, create one powerful affirmation or mantra and repeat it over and over all day long. You can clean your house or work out while you repeat your affirmation". An example of an affirmation creation would be "I am a Butterfinger, I allow low vibrations to slip through my mind and fingers"! You can always create an affirmation that works best for you. Please share with me the affirmation you created in order to become a Butterfinger.

Don't Eat A Butterfinger, Be One Release Reminder

» With weight release, we have to be butterfingers, at a certain point, we have to let food slip through our fingers

» Being a Butterfinger means portion control

» An example of an affirmation creation would be "I am a Butterfinger, I allow low vibrations to slip through my mind and fingers"

"There Comes A Time In Every Man's Life"

Let me grab you by the hand for this "peace" of advice. So long as you are human "there comes a time in every man's life" where you will retort, "what the fuck!" While this may not be your exact sentiment nor verbal expression you use, energetically speaking we all have experienced heart crushing emotions which "makes our heart sick". This evil, vile, soul ache I'm refencing here is hope deferred. Man oh man, do I tussle with Releasing hope deferred. Centuries ago, the poet of Proverbs quickly surmised that hope deferred "makes the heart sick". To make it plain, think of a sick heart, both physically and mentally-no thank you to both. Consider when your heart is broken from any facet of life. What are your thoughts, words, and movement (behavior)-in that order?

Since we are Releasing our excess physical weight, in times of trouble, how fast do you, like me, reach for fast food? How fast do you make up the slimmest names for yourself in a situation where you exhibited you were human? These examples, where a nasty habit I assumed was happiness or at least a pacifier. Oh yes, a sick heart produces even sicker behavior. Here's why, "when storm clouds gather around you they hide your hope. That hope deferred creates an unhealthy climate around you that dictates the stormy forecast of your relationships." However, now that we are Releasing All In Love And Trust we cannot climb in this hope-deferred bed and pull the covers over our heads, Release.

Lifestyle Release Tip #1
"Thank God For Granting Me This Moment Of Clarity"

Focus in on the last word of the above quote, it states relationships, s, a plural, more than one relationship. This Lifestlye Release Tip, rose to the surface of my mind, because you may encounter an opportunity of growth with "Sister Such-And-Such" at church. Please don't hone in on "Sister Such-And-Such" at church, yes she gives you ample reasons to holla out a number of unruly sayings, however, we are Releasing our belief in hope deferred so any external factors are not real to us anymore, so therefore they don't exist, including "Sister Such-And-Such" or any presence we may to misdirect our anger, oops! I mean evolving toward.

"Time Don't Go Back, It Moves Forward"
-Shawn Carter

Do not meander on ugly thoughts, they will take you down – shit yeah its real, however even greater is your Higher Power and the higher power that resides within you. Look over the horizon of your life and smile. "You must learn to deal powerfully with failure". Say huh, say who, say what? Yes, you are not above failure, from parables of old to Greek Mythology we see, read, and hear, of empires collapsing and rich men becoming pulpers, failure is a part of the ebb and flow of life, yet you have to deal with it powerfully. Failure is what leads to your life and weight release success.

Be clear, I'm not negating the soul pain that failure welcomes, nonetheless you must deal with the circumstances as a King or Queen would. Please remember, heavy is the head that wears the crown, unwelcomed situations will come about. A delay or failure was not just for the greats and noble kings in your favorite movie or novel. At the end of the day, "time don't go back it moves forward", Mercy said no for the moment. While this truth and salve may taste like pig liver cuisine, you and I must Release and believe there is a greater purpose at play.

During my adventures as a classroom educator, teachers often attended what was termed a Professional Learning Community, PLC. One of the goals of a PLC was to discuss effective strategies for the classroom. I liken this experience to soldiers heading out to battle and when they return discuss the strategies that produced desirable results as well as the areas of growth that lie within yourself and the classroom. Absorb the following battlefield strategies to deal powerfully with failure.

Genesis
Full Accountability

"Take full accountability for your actions or the ones you failed to tackle". It happened! Yes, you ate an extra piece of cake or 3, yes, you hissed at your co-workers and kids, yes, you were fascinated by the water cooler office gossip, it was you, take accountability. Writer Allison Fallon penned a post titled "The Positive Benefits of Failure" in it Fallon fills us in on the extensive effects of no accountability. When we try to pass the buck – when we make excuses for ourselves, blame other people, or try to avoid the natural consequences of our actions, the results are the opposite. Our failure snowballs into more failure" not only will a lack of accountability cause strife in your life, situations become immense not decreasing in size and nature.

Pardon yourself from this faux reality. Here's the truth, after you take ownership, your heart is still beating, someone still loves you, you didn't lose a limb, no natural disasters like a volcanic eruption took place. Life did not stop happening and neither will you.

Shhh! Can You Keep A Secret?
There Is No Secret

For this Release I read multiple sources of information on the cult, I mean world of dieting. Here's what I found out, shhh, can you keep a secret? There is no secret diet. Hundreds of research institutions and others devoted to the weight release cause conducted interviews with individuals who have successful weight release on a long-term basis, here's what they discovered, "there really, truly is no one best diet. The experts I spoke to all emphasized that science has now shown us, pretty much unequivocally, that all diets-low fat, low carb, Weight Watchers, Atkins, etc. – have the same modest results in the long run, no matter their macronutrient composition".

Diets run the gamut Releasers, meaning, be it Weight Watchers or Mediterranean Diet the common thread will always be ourselves. With Releasing, we no longer believe, that we are the common denominator and exception to the rule. Here's the solution, grab some motivation and set some goals. Don't go, "oh lord, another task"! This is as simple as getting in at least your minimum number of daily steps or falling back from the vending machine sodas for the first 3 days of next week, baby step goals, make a world of a difference and keep you motivated. This is essential for long-term results. At this time in your life, be it personal or professional, South Beach diet or Releasing All In Love And Trust, make sure you are motivated and set goals. Perhaps you already set some goals and not achieving the results you would like to receive, now would be the time to make adjustments to your goals based on the results you learned from "dealing with failure powerfully". Here's the strategy to help you deal with failure powerfully, please remember, in order to evolve you must look at your life through the lenses of data, statistics of sorts. Therefore, in order to make the proper behavior modifications, you must view your life and results as "data revealed, emotion removed". You must view your life as data and remove the emotion because you will continuously beat yourself up and plant your feet further in an undesirable circumstance. Remove the emotion, its causing you to delay and stumble, stay focused on the data, that way you are able to clearly see what behavior has to be Released.

Distorted Perception of Success

We've all been there, you've just finished viewing a film that has you as high-spirited as its momentum. Your motivation is at a premium, and aware of all the necessary evils, you are prepared to be mighty in battle to fulfill your heart's desire. Armed with vigor and ambition you create a plan as follows. In the blink of an eye you will discover a cure for all mankind. Next, you hop a plane to East Africa where you will overthrow a dynasty with one swift glide of a sword. All the while earning your doctorates in Biochemistry. Let me not fail to mention, this was safely completed within the timeframe of 2 weeks. Sounds legit and doable? Sounds more like a distorted perception of success. Julia Belluz, wrote a delightful article titled Surprisingly simple tips from 20 experts about how to lose (Release) weight and keep it off, Julia's #4 tip was "Diets often fail because of unreasonable expectations. People who go on diets often set themselves up for failure by expecting results too quickly, picking a plan that either doesn't fit with their lifestyle or is impossible to maintain."

Let's start from scratch with our distorted perceptions. Yes, the protagonist was victorious in battle despite surmounting obstacles. However, let's not skip over the portion of the film that included preparation time. Think Rocky Balboa (all 5 or 6, wth, wtf), drinking egg yoks, running uphill in adverse weather and training from sunup to sun down, with the assistance of a supreme team around him. Yes, honey, that grind, gristle, and hustle is the preparation time for success. Here's the juiciness and instant success, that grind and hustle is a temporary process wrapped around an innate, magical gift that you possessed all along.

Like Puff, Tax Brackets Aside

Now that we are Releasing distorted views on success, let's get to the bottom of a few things. Long before our existence, the Universe established Law and Order. Hell, I wish this book wrote itself over four years ago and slapped my name on the cover, yet, payment is required up front from the Universe or the Higher Power you claim to believe. Let's take a moment to apply this mental Release, to our physical Release.

One of my several, elite, Mentors In My Mind (MIMM) is Sean "Puffy" Combs, or Diddy. In 2003, Puffy ran the New York City Marathon for children's charities and New York City public schools. Do you think the Universe cared he was a multi-millionaire in the flesh? No, he had to physically train and prepare just like you or I. You bet, he had to modify his diet and adjust his schedule just to name a few. Diddy's damn near billion-dollar's worth ass, had to Release negative thoughts and emotions so he could literally get his Rocky on. Want another reason to stay the path? Regardless of Puffy's money, assistants, and trainers, he "developed severe tendonitis in his right knee" and quoted as saying "I definitely wanted to stop." Despite the luxuries afforded from Diddy's hard work, we are able to witness that no one is exempt from the process.

Here's The Joy, Nobody Taught Us How To Succeed

While we may have had the illest game plan from start to completion in a matter of our favorite heroic movie, in reality, we discovered the truth-it's only a movie, a fictional motion picture, somewhat based on the truth. The process was diminished for time's sake-insert here-no pun intended. Here's the joy, nobody taught us how to succeed so of course we would naturally perceive our heart's desire would be attained during a movies worth time frame, and not the movies Gladiator, Malcolm X, or Titanic. Success is creating and completing OURSELVES, the Balboa experience within our lives. Quick note, while your genre, heart's desire, or experience may not require you to drink egg yoks like a professional athlete, mentally, ALL have to prepare in this manner, once again, no one is exempt from the process.

Here's how we make the connection to succeed, pay special attention to how Rocky or Puff, the physical man, responds during a training session. What I mean here is, their bodies perspire heavily from its synchronized movement, recall Diddy's tendonitis from training?

Rocky, for example, must be offered words of encouragement-sometimes in tough love. Above all, like you and me, both men must RECEIVE and ADHERE to instruction, remember how I mentioned they had and have supreme teams around them? -THIS IS HOW YOU SUCCEED

No My Love, You Don't Know

Thank God we are all smart, THANK GOD! There are worlds that exist outside of your window and not just the window you peer through from your place of shelter, even your mental window-the view through which you guide your life. Cultures, lifestyles, and beliefs dominate our actions and intentions. Thus creating a society where most adhere unconsciously to these beliefs no matter how fruitful or fatal. Here's the thing, you and I must encounter these individuals, for you and I are one of them. With that said, all have been equipped with The Universal capacity to navigate the forest of culture, understand the jungle of belief, and observe the safari of lifestyle.

Baby, you don't know, however you are smart enough to learn, understand, and observe so that you may know(ledge). Here's where I'm going with this, these are your first steps in Releasing All in Love and Trust, liken this experience to being a first generation graduate, or the first in your family to purchase a home. Hence you being the first to ... You, no one else, are evolving, so you are going to become informed on every level. This means you are learning and more times than not, on this journey you will have to go it alone-just you and your Higher Power. Simply put, there is a first time for everything and you and I are on that first-time journey. "Discouragement is inevitable when you do not know "how" and "what" it takes to succeed. Success will require, amongst other things, courage, perspiration, faith, patience, quality learning." When we as individuals begin to Release All, it becomes our personal journey-solo. In order to evolve, we must destroy some of the first-time journey perceptions that impede us from receiving that which we yearn for.

"10 Years To Become An Overnight Success"

In an "Aha Moment" text titled How To Be An Overnight Success, the CEO and Founder of Rodial, Maria Hatzistefanis lamented that when we observe an "overnight success" more than likely, what we are observing is "overnight exposure. I have yet to find a brand that was created overnight and had a sustainable business model. Overnight success is really just overnight exposure. And to get your business that exposure, you are going to have to keep on pushing." Just as sure as seeds planted in the soil must take time to grow and blossom, so it is with ourselves, we must allow this Release and flow. What is funny to note, as an illustration of the process, Maria went on to explain how she "changed careers three times before I started my own business and I was fired from my last job".

In an interview given by one of my favorite artist and MIMM, Mr. Carter himself, Jay-Z, he explained how his first album did not drop until he was 26 or 27 years old, not to mention, the stream of no's he and his team had to endure before they created their own Yes. Talking about patience for the seed to develop and manifest within the soil! Being about the same age as Jigga Man when I completed my undergraduate studies, I was aware of the required patience when you want something to happen yesterday, this energetic connection was real and present within me. By the way, Maria's overnight success came by way of 18 years. Here's what's dope about 26, 27, or however young you may be, the process still has to go down and it will all be worth it. Jay-Z is a clear vivid example of this. How many decades later, and in how many ways are we still chanting his name? Even better, are his own words, as to why you have to stay the 10 years to overnight success road -"Ain't no such thing as a ugly billionaire, I'm cute!"

Overnight Success To-Do List

- Stay The Course – The going gets tough-please remember Like Puff, Tax Brackets Aside

- Focus on you and your brand, not lower vibrations, the process still has to go down and you are standing in the way by focusing on the wrong variables.

- ***Measure Success By Obedience – "We often look to numbers and outward achievements, but God sees things differently. Stay focused on obedience to what God has told you to do, and don't compare yourself with others. God sees your worth and rejoices in it."

I MISSSS YOUUUU!!!! #FUCKcancer

"Houston, We Have A Problem"
"Phone Home"

Where were you when Tom Hanks, playing the role of astronaut Jim Lovell, phoned home by saying "Houston, we have a problem"? While we know the astronaut manning the Apollo 13 did not fashion those words in that exact order, we got his drift, a situation, out of he and the crew's control occurred. Place yourself in the same position, you are off and running with your weight release or special project at work and as life would have it, an unforeseen circumstance has now divided your attention. Here's the thing, as long as you are living, life will happen, and you will have to phone home. Yes it may initially feel weird, and down right uncomfortable yet we have goals here to achieve and hearts desires to manifest on the physical plane, so we do what we have to do!

We were either taught directly or indirectly that independence was key in all areas of lives, this belief only leads to continual failure. Do you know the team behind Lebron James and not just on the court? In addition to shouting out his wife Savannah for holding it down, he has agents, assistants, PR staff, trainers, the list goes on and on-this is what it takes, an entire team to produce the world's top athlete.

Didn't want to leave you hanging out there with your independent news flash, here is some awesome news. "When we fail, we send out flares (often without realizing it) to those who matter most: friends, family, and close colleagues who can offer assistance or simply lend a sympathetic ear. The process strengthens our support system and builds a network of resources to help us succeed next time". "Oh what needless pain we bear"-remember that hymnal, take it to your Higher Power, and hit up your resources, vent, express what you are truly feeling unapologetically. Please Remember-"No Man's An Island Peninsula Maybe".

Never Better Than Them
"Who She Is, Is Sorry"
-Iyanla Vanzant

During the early seasons of Iyanla Fix My Life on one of the episodes, Iyanla was explaining to the daughters of a wayward mother that one of the reasons the daughters are not able to accept, receive, and observe a true apology from their mother is because "who she is sorry, her whole being is sorry" this is why her actions return to dust and no progression has been obtained. This aha moment proved monumental for me, while I was walking around taking the actions of others personal, here's what I discovered-who they are is sorry. It wouldn't matter what went on or who did it, when an individual is hurt and refusing to properly seek attention for their hurt, then sorry is sure to follow. Anything they touch or interact with will be treated in like-sorry. Here is where I am headed, when you are seeking out that support system during those hard times you are going to run into people, where, who they are is sorry, their whole being is sorry, yes, this will be a shock and surprise but my loves there are people who never want to see you doing better than them because who they are is sorry. You must choose wisely with whom you vent your concerns to, everyone is not available within that frame, and your success reflects an even greater light on their lack of progression. Seek the proper people and places, were you will receive the support you need. Now that we are Releasing All In Love And Trust, we know, we are worthy of that level of love and support.

Hard Times Require Furious Dancing
-Alice Walker

Thanks to the profound being Alice Walker we have been given and now receive a weight release and life strategy for the hard times that may arrive in our life-furious dancing. Be it ballet, tap, or your own mean two-step, you have to whip out your Soul Trains best dance moves. Honey, let me be the first to tell you that I am Releasing two left feet, however you still have to get up and groove and I will join you with my two left feet (that I am Releasing). "Movement and music are both powerful antidotes for stress. Exercise of any kind helps to alleviate pent-up anxiety and releases feel-good endorphins. Music helps to bring our emotions to the forefront, enabling us to work them out".

As I bring this section to a close, I've gathered a collection of songs that get me through the hard times and there beats require furious dancing. From gospel, R&B, to hip-hop, use these songs to arise from whatever ashes you are Releasing. As a matter-of-fact, feel free to collect your own or add to my selections.

Playlist For Furious Dancing

Gospel

- Trust In God By The Winans

- Don't Worry By Commissioned

- Come To Me By Angie & Debbie Winans

- That's When You Blessed Me By L.A. Mass Choir

Rhythm & Blues

- September By Earth, Wind, & Fire

- Get On Up By Jodeci

- Encore By Cheryl Lynn

- Back To Life By Soul II Soul

Hip-Hop

- Stressed Out By A Tribe Called Quest Featuring Faith Evans

- Girls Dem Sugar By Beenie Man Featuring Mya

- Feels So Good By Remy Ma Featuring Ne-Yo

- Peaceful By Slim Thug (He's A Whole Snack)

Other Types of Furious Dancing

- Take accountability for your actions or the ones you failed to tackle

- Avoid any particle of lowly – Do not meander on ugly thoughts

- Speak like a pirate – no one really has to know- deny all accusations should the subject arise

Pirate Terms to Get You Going

» Begad – By God

» Belay – Stop that. "Belay that talk!" would mean "Shut up!" – Especially to the ugly, nasty, thoughts we tote around

» Blimey! – An exclamation of surprise.

» Gangway! – "Get out of my way!"

» No quarter! – Surrender will not be accepted. Especially to our weight release and life goals

Bite Your Tongue

Releasers, we have arrived! This lifestyle transformation has been wonderful with you. As we enter into the final phase of our Release, we are now crossing some T's and dotting our I's. Our portion, of this whole, is required because we are ever-evolving. Yes, biting your tongue is required on the path of evolution. I know, why would something so painful, with a light mix of torture be recommended? How many times are we able to recount the disturbing moment we bit our tongue. Even the aftermath of biting your tongue is awful. The ducking and dodging when you eat, the disdain or comfort of your tongue depending on what you drink. And don't even think of the double murder of biting your tongue twice in the same spot, just brutal! I'll move along this is not pleasant reminiscing.

Biting your tongue is recommended in more places than one. The ever-classy Victoria Beckham, VB, even vouches for the painful act. "In 2016, Victoria included some marriage advice in a letter addressed to her 18 year old self, published in British Vogue. 'In marriage: have patience. Bite your tongue. Be supportive. And preserve a bit of mystique".

Self-Love First

Here's the thing, and I will use VB as my first example. Do you think she enjoys biting her tongue? How about this one, do you think she wakes up each morning stating "I hope I get to bite my tongue today, as a matter of fact, I'll look for ways to bite my tongue!" I would say a firm no, to both of those questions. However we are made free, and love ourselves first. Imagine the ill-will and lack of joy that would proceed in our life if we responded, with snazz, to everything that came our way, especially with our loved ones.

Since we are all human, just think if you had an individual that you shared your world with, who never bit their tongue with you, you'd be over it pretty damn quick. And I am not letting you off the hook that easy, that's the same love we have to apply to ourselves. Biting your tongue also applies to you, yes, you, are you are reading correctly. Our mental can create and hurl some pretty nasty, mean, comments to ourselves. You have to bite your tongue with your own self, mind, and thoughts. We have to condition our minds to truth.

When To Bite Your Tongue
Acts of Self-Love

Now that we have cleared some truths out of the way, let us discuss when to bite your tongue. Since external factors do exist, there are times when you may experience feelings of a low vibration. "But feeling angry is not bad. And allowing ourselves to consciously express that anger is actually very healthy, both emotionally and physically. Pent-up anger makes us sick. Healthy expression is good".

Here's what's good about biting your tongue, you are not denying the situation nor your feelings, we now love ourselves first to ensure the best outcome for our lives. Here are 3 scenarios of when biting your tongue is actually self-love.

Walk with me for a moment, because it's the human experience, we arise in the morning and our mental temperature is tepid so in our Monica voice, we declare "it's one of them days!" Now that we address our emotions and do not suppress them, we acknowledge, "when our emotions are running high". While the first may seem like a given, I can recall several professional situations where I should have bit my tongue even if I drew blood. "Speaking up in the workplace when your emotions are running high usually never pans out well. More often than not, you end up saying something you regret and ultimately make the situation that much worse".

"When you don't have anything productive to offer" to a situation, is another example of how biting your tongue works out best for you once again. You may want to contribute to a situation however this is the time we reach back to our W.A.I.T. strategies, Why Am I Talking (Gabrielle Bernstein) and What Am I Thinking. Once you receive your answers from both you will know how to proceed in a given situation. "However, there's really no point in speaking up if you don't actually have anything of substance to say. So, whether it's a piece of criticism that's more brutal than constructive or a point that's completely irrelevant to what's being discussed, you're better off keeping quiet when you don't have anything valuable to offer. Trust me, everybody will appreciate it".

My final example of where biting your tongue is an act of self-love is "when the conversation turns to gossip". From church, to your neighbor, down to the kid's beautician, we all can find places to receive the latest gossip. Here's the thing, how fast would we run to that gossip if we knew the latest 411 was about us, and the information was not a rumor at all, it was the truth? I bet our priorities would shift, and we would not be as swift to be apart of the unofficial New

York Times. "Participating –even with just a seemingly innocent comment –can easily come back to bite you. So keep your mouth shut and politely remove yourself from the conversation".

How To Properly Bite Your Tongue

As I have stated, biting your tongue is not about applying pain to your life, it's actually the opposite, and in the direction of love, the love where you put yourself first. Knowing how to express your emotions is the proper way to bite your tongue. In an article that I recommend, 11 Steps To Express Your Emotions, I will provide you with the first 2 steps because biting your tongue may require spilt-second thinking. "Identify the emotion and the feeling. When something changes in your body from reacting to something, either external or something within your own thoughts, you should ask yourself: What am I feeling? What physical symptoms am I experiencing? What is the cause? Why is it happening now?"

Next, you are encouraged to "learn to recognize your feelings. Once you have detected your emotions and feelings, you have to analyze the sensation that it creates within you. It is useful to know what signs and gestures betray you. Try to make a list of all of those emotions and what exactly it is that physically gives them away".

A Treat For Biting Your Tongue

I didn't want to leave you upset with me, so I added this treat, for the times that you do bite your tongue, yet you need some additional Release. "Use the tennis racket method. Make sure you use a pillow that can handle the force of you hitting it with a tennis racket. If you do this, pause when you are finished and notice what you feel in your body." Own a tennis racket? If no, the thrift store has one with your name written on it. This does not have to be an expensive tennis racket, politely head down to your local thrift store to purchase a racket and a durable pillow. Your field trip to the thrift store is also a great time to explore your sense of fashion, be chic in your selection of pillows and tennis rackets.

Weight Release

Let's face the scenario of biting our tongue through weight release. Here's the thing Releasers, we all set out with good intentions, yet sometimes our actions and the circumstances play out totally different. When it comes to food the same goes, we have to bite our tongue, when we know that our stomach is saying satisfied. Also let's not lie to ourselves and say even though I'm going to Auntie Such and Such's home, I'll be fine, regardless of the neighborhood lining up around the block for her potato salad. Releasers, bite your tongue, do not go over there, Skype or FaceTime. Since we love ourselves first we take the proper precautions. You have been given some dope strategies throughout the book, so please remember that if you do attend Auntie Such's cookout, spilt your plate in half and save the rest for later.

When To Bite Your Tongue Release Reminder

» Bite your tongue with your own self, mind, and thoughts. We have to Release and condition our minds to truth

» Biting your tongue is not denying the situation nor your feelings, we now love ourselves first to ensure the best outcome for our lives

» Bite your tongue, when we know that your stomach is saying satisfied

Chapter 10

Fish Out Of Water

Fish Out of Water
To All My Clothes & Full-Figured Sections I've Visited

As you begin to Release your mental weight, your shape compliments the mental adjustments. You will begin to find yourself slipping right into those pair of jeans that once took a dancing act to get into. Those pit and pendulum arms of yours, will cease its motions and in my case, some of my shoes got a little bigger, or did they? As time moves along you will come to terms with your true beauty and take the love steps forward to clear out your wardrobe and replace those old thoughts, feelings, and clothing, where they belong –in the past. Once again, I will state that my mother was my champion and trainer with moving forward in purchasing the appropriate fitting clothing, otherwise "catch a grip Haven, the past is over, you are fine, get your fine ass in a store, and get the proper garments that reflect your fineness"! I'm saying the same to you, get in that store and allow your fine ass to reflect. Here is where you will become a fish out of water!

To all my clothes and full-figured sections, I've visited, there's nothing more fulfilling and beautiful than the experience of walking into the foreign land of your favorite store, picking out your size and it fits like a hand in a glove, mercy, this is a wonderful, lifelong dream. Internally I felt that of an Olympian, when they receive their medals and begin crying uncontrollably, yes, that way.

As Long As You Keep Your Head To The Sky
Be Optimistic

Here's why there may be some internal conflict with accepting your new reality and normalcy. "The tension between the inner self and outer self is common in the modern world. Each of us is tugged in multiple directions every day and our actions and behaviors do not always align with our core values as a result". For my women readers, we know all about how we are subconsciously taught to be everything at once, this is an example I see in women across color lines, age, finances, married or single. You have to know that you are not totally responsible for your resistance to this part of the process. "This external world can be demanding, leaving little time for you to consider whether what is taking place on the outside of your life matches what you ultimately desire on the inside".

Yes, Releasers, it's that inside, our dear pal subconscious, that has us wearing size 18/20 pants to work, when I really wore about a 12, those pants flowed on me like a maxi dress, and no, that was not a good thing, as I am laughing and writing this in a much sounder mind, I can totally see the driving force behind my mother's behavior. Healing is wonderful, and the experience will allow you to view the universe as it truly is – the Garden of Eden, please remember there was supposedly a tree of good and evil in the garden, it has been advised that you stay clear of this tree. However, since I wrote this book and you are reading it, that's an indication that we did not take that advice to heart and need to listen up –you have all this garden over here, do not go over there!

"The inner self is about what can't be seen: feelings, intuition, values, beliefs, personality, thoughts, emotions, fantasies, spirituality, desire, and purpose". Often times Releasers, we have faced situations where our feelings had to be suffocated. This suffocation allowed a false belief to form, no more, false means that it is not true or real.

"Problems begin when the inner self and outer self are in conflict or out of balance". Your beauty inside and out is real and its' knocking on all your doors to come out and be released.

Benefits to releasing and accepting our fish out of water status plays a part on our weight release as well, when we reject certain notions in our lives, it causes stress to rise. "Increased levels of cortisol can not only make you crave unhealthy food, but excess nervous energy can often cause you to eat more than you normally would. How many times have you found yourself scouring the kitchen for a snack, or absently munching on junk food when you're stressed, but not really hungry?"

Here is where we tap into our Sounds of Blackness voices and sing out with them, "as long as you keep your head to the sky, you can win", yes, optimistic, your Higher Power knows, you were not bought this far to be left as a fish out of water, it's a portion of the path that we all must walk.

Let's Release our fears and embrace our fish out of water status with optimism and a firm belief in ourselves. "Negative events are more likely to roll off your back, and positive events affirm your belief in yourself, your ability to make good things happen now and, in the future, and in the goodness of life". As we move along to our next section, let's take some quiet time within our day, to ask ourselves "does your current life require you to stifle deeply held values?"

Develop A Love of Learning
No, Not Advanced Physics

Now that we are embracing our fish out of water status we can begin to learn how to keep from flip-flopping about in our new element. "Being a fish out of water in a new culture is an amazing experience. Every day, every relationship, every interaction is an opportunity for learning and growth." This is us now, we have released our mental fallacies and developed a love of learning. Be clear I am not advising you to take a class in advanced physics, developing a love of learning is taking a class in an area that you know will draw giggles from your friends and family, that's the love of learning I want you to explore.

Here's where I want to bring a band out or grab a bull-horn to capture your attention. Human connection is critical, valuable, and needs to be emphasized. Do not allow the choices that others make -screaming out independence- play a role in your life. I will also say that technology can cause us to become withdrawn as well, there are so many ways that you can connect with a love one now a days, human connection can be very limited and the space to interact on that level has to be drawn out and intentional in our lives.

When we expand our minds through a love of learning, you never know who you will meet and establish a connection. There are individuals from vast worlds and places with countless stories and experiences to share and teach. "The purpose of self-development is to allow us to be more helpful to others. The more we learn and grow, the better able we are to serve humanity in meaningful ways". As a side note, and a networking tip, this is one way that a person

228

who knows everybody, meets everybody!

Fish Out of Water
In Water

Naturally if you are a fish out of water, you are going to want some in-water navigation. There's no point in dipping your frustrations in a river of false thoughts, instead we can gather ways to swim the friendly seas. "What helps people to survive in unfamiliar waters is the skill of code switching".

If you were raised by a black woman, then you have your doctorates in code switching, oh, you still don't know what I mean. Think about how your mother acted with her church friends versus her friends from around the way. Think about how your mother talked on the phone at work versus home, how about when your mom was on official business outside of the home and the stern look she would give you, if your behavior was not up to par. These are examples of code switching, "code switching may mean changing your style of language; it always means changing your style of engagement, learning the 'house rules' or cultural expectations of wherever you are". Yes, my loves, in order to Release fish out of water, you have to be able to code switch. Now don't get nervous because there are some simple, non-intrusive ways that you are able to code switch and not make a fool out of yourself. You also must let go because your blood sugar is at play. "Prolonged stress can alter your blood sugar levels, causing mood swings and fatigue. Too much stress has been linked to metabolic syndrome, a cluster of health concerns that can lead to greater health problems like heart attacks and diabetes". To keep you in better health and releasing weight, I'm going to leave you with 5 quick tips to Release fish out of water.

"Observe what others are doing", this may seem like a simple step, yet it may take time for you to absorb what you are viewing. Take the time to soak in the scene, it's one of the first keys to being wise. The flip side of the coin to this tip, is to remember to observe those that are experiencing success. Not everyone you come across will be on the level on your heart's desire, so you have to make sure your observation reflects the direction in which you would like to head.

"Try it out", here's the part of the journey where your vulnerability is at play, because we no longer ride the sidelines in fear. Once you have observed, its time to engage in some calculated risk. Here's the thing, now that you are code switching and observing, the fear is not as great as you imagine. Please remember not to dive in but to set yourself up for success. Practice baby steps with this tip by beginning with simple then moving on to more complex experiences.

"Get a cultural guide", at the end of the day, we all need help, our experiences may be new to us however they are not new to life. There is a mentor willing to share their expertise with you and lend an ear for you to vent. As with observations please make sure that your mentor has experienced the ebb and flow within their lives and still attained success.

"Increase awareness", you may feel as if you need a subscription to a popular medical journey in order to increase your awareness, that's not the truth, honor yourself by subscribing to 1 blogger in your field and commit to reading at least one of their post a week. Also "learn the codes of those in power and use them effectively".

"Reassess and realign", this is the beauty of life especially when you are willing to learn, you discover that there are no such things as mistakes, you realign according to your results.

Fish Out of Water Release Reminder

»   Embrace fish out of water status

»   Take some quiet time within your day, to ask yourself "does your current life require you to stifle deeply held values?"

»   Get your fine ass in a store, so you can purchase the proper garments that reflect your fineness"!

»   "Problems begin when the inner self and outer self are in conflict or out of balance"- check in with yourself

»   Develop a love of learning by taking a class in an area that you know will draw giggles from your friends and family

»   Code Switch, there are simple, non-intrusive ways that you are able to code switch and not make a fool out of yourself.

Friends
How Many Of Us Have Them

Whodini, put us up on a lot of game, when he posed the question in his hit Friends. I'll ask the question again myself, friends, how many of us have them? By now in your weight release journey, you are becoming aware of the friends that you truly possess. I know that this revelation may be bittersweet, soon, it will become all sweet, sweeter than honey to be exact.

Here's the thing, to no fault of our own, we can create unrealistic expectations for not just ourselves but extend this treatment to others. That's why it's important to understand that there is no limit to love, however what are your expectations of love and who are you placing them upon? Not to be the Fun Police, yet, lets pause for a moment and think about how we as women can get touchy when it comes to planning a wedding, notice I said planning a wedding, spoke nothing of the marriage that is supposed to be forever. You know how it goes, who is the maid of honor, who is going to stand where, what in the world got a hold of that bridesmaid dress? You know, the vital aspect of marriage, lol! Yes, we can extend our expectations to some pretty vast places.

Now I know that I started out by asking you how many friends you have, yet I am focusing on you, here's why, you have to be your own best friend first before you can extend this level of intimacy and love to anyone else. One of the ways to Release unrealistic expectations, is to check in with yourself and observe what you feel is love and how you display your love. This will place you on the path of friendship. To be clear, while your engines need to be up and running, you do need to be aware of the different types of friendship and where people fit into those spaces in your life. This is applicable so you can create the proper expectations.

"Four Levels of Friendship"

Many moons ago and as a Christmas present, my Mom brought me the book Friendships, Avoiding the Ones That Hurt, Finding the Ones That Heal. I never imagined how eye-opening the book would be. Here's why it's cause-worthy to read text of this nature. You may honestly be under the impression that you are an amazing friend and that friendship etiquette is a given, and this "friendship etiquette" is all based on your perception –WRONG!

There's much to learn and know about friendships, which is why we previously created unrealistic expectations for ourselves and others. Jeff Wickwire, the author of the book, states "generally speaking, there are four levels of friendship. Acquaintances, casual friendships, close friendships, and intimate friendships (best friends).God has placed a friend-shaped hole in every soul".

Now is the time to become informed. As you get to know the different levels of friendship, you will begin to place your friendships in their proper place, your expectations are shifting towards reality because you are learning friendship, and how it applies to your world.

The Sister Circle Will Always Be Unbroken

Negative Female Friends

While this is a topic that I would rather not explore, it must be addressed because we love ourselves first. In the past we may have brushed off a friend's jealousy do to our own insecurities, but no more, we now address a portion of our soul that we allowed to be previously battered. "Women tend to be more sensitive and body conscious (blame the culture and the media) which often leads to this negative behavior, even if they have no real, valid problem with you at all".

There were several instances in the early stages of my weight release where I was questioned on whether or not I had surgery, as a matter of fact, a sweet individual asked if me and my mother had surgery. You are able to ask most that know me and definitely prior to Releasing All In Love And Trust, I was a pretty transparent individual so if I was to have surgery, there would have been no problem with me speaking up and saying that I did so. Here's the thing, "in some ways, your weight loss (release) becomes a symbol of their inability to accomplish their goals, so they begin to act resentful –or even mean– oftentimes without even realizing they are doing so, says Christian Holle, PhD, an assistant professor of psychology at William Patterson University".

My research for this book opened my eyes to the ways we as humans' function especially out of fear. We can become so hurt and tangled in our emotions and beliefs, our actions may not truly reflect our feelings. For example, learning of "thin privilege" through If You Want To Lose Weight, Don't Tell Your Friends", blew my mind. "For women in particular, the slimmer you are, the more privileged you are in your love life, career, and economic situation. Studies have shown that both men and women consider women to be more attractive when thin (and actually under a healthy weight range)".

The stakes can run very high if we allow them to, so we have to stay clear of any form of negativity not just with our friends, because family members can through darts as well. However, now that we are Releasing, we take responsibility for our actions. "There's also self-sabotage. If you know that going to certain restaurants or buying particular foods will tempt you, avoid them –and stay away from triggering situations or people that are likely to make you want to stress –eat". One step in the direction of discovering negative friends would be to consider their actions prior to your weight release. Now that we are healing and Releasing, the simple is being made wise in us, so we recognize previous situations for what they were -an act of jealousy.

Just so you won't delete most of your Facebook friends and block those who missed your birthday, I want to be clear that this will not be all of your friends, and you may have a friend who just has a moment. "Your friend may be expressing weight loss jealousy because they're discouraged about their own weight loss attempts. If you think that's the case, offer some encouragement". These are not the friends and family members that you kick to the curb.

Shhh! Don't Tell Nobody

Earlier I mentioned an article, If You Want To Lose Weight, Don't Tell Your Friends, the author explains that "your efforts to reach a healthier weight, and your reasons for dieting, are nobody's business but your own". Her suggestion was not just about your friends, they are for you as well. "For one thing, if you tell people your goals, you're less likely to be motivated or to put in as much effort to succeed. Change is often incremental, not dramatic –especially when it comes to dieting". Remember Flossie's words to us "you scatter your forces by talking about your affairs. Don't discuss your business with your family. Silence is golden!"

"Don't Be A Weight Release Crusader"

Wanting all things to be equal I do feel that I need to share a phase within weight release that we as Releasers tend to overlook because we our overjoyed with our new lifestyles. However here is how we are really coming off. You remember Richard Simmons, Sweating to the Oldies, try him, and first thing in the morning –NO THANK YOU! Be clear, I am not stating this is how you come off when you speak to someone in the morning, this is you 24/7, no matter

236

the time of day. Trust me, there are people that are happy for you and even want to make the change themselves, we just have to give everybody their time and space. As time moves along you will begin to balance out your feelings and methods of spreading the good news. Don't worry, all is not lost, you never know what the next person is going through and your crusade may be just the thing to pick them up and pull them of their temporary rotten circumstances. Continue to keep the fire burning!

My Every-tings

Beyonce, Cindy Crawford, Pepsi Commercial
Not Everyone Wants To See You Down

You're that Beyonce, Cindy Crawford Pepsi commercial now, yes, you glow and move like their flow. Not everyone wants to see you down, "focus on the positive energy that will be coming your way. You may even share your story and inspire countless others to start their weight loss (release) journey too. You may lose people you thought of as friends but for every negative person that leaves your life, a positive one could pop up". With life, weight release included you will have to focus on the beautiful and positive and know that nothing else exist. You can focus on the negative people and situations that have caused you hell on earth or you can focus on that which brings you peace, beauty, and joy. The latter is overflowing and what you were put here to experience. Please allow this beauty to overflow within, you will see the mental and physical beauty that is abounding, all around you, give it a go!

Friends Release Reminder

» To no fault of our own, we can create unrealistic expectations for not just ourselves but extend this treatment to others

» Check-in with yourself and observe what you feel is love and how you display your love

» "Stay away from triggering situations or people that are likely to make you want to stress –eat"

» "Your efforts to reach a healthier weight, and your reasons for dieting, are nobody's business but your own"

Release Me To A Review

Now that you have *Released All In Love & Trust,* Thank You for leaving me a 5-Star Review on a book platform of your choice. I look forward to replying to your thoughts and the lessons you carried away from the book. Please remember, you don't lose weight, you *Release it!*

We'll chat soon!

Love,
Haven

Made in the USA
Columbia, SC
13 September 2020